THE *NEW* COLLEGE OF TRIVIAL KNOWLEDGE

By the same author:

Geometry for Teachers

Lessons in Essential Mathematics: Book I

Lessons in Essential Mathematics: Book II

Lessons in College Algebra with Trigonometry

Lessons in College Algebra

The College of Trivial Knowledge

THE *NEW* COLLEGE OF TRIVIAL KNOWLEDGE

Robert A. Nowlan, Ph.D.

Quill • New York

Library of Congress Cataloging in Publication Dat

Nowlan, Robert A.
The new college of trivial knowledge.
1. Questions and answers. I. Title. II. Title: Trivial knowledge.
AG195.N63 1985 031′.02 84–24914
ISBN 0-688-04706-8 (pbk).

Printed in the United States of America

First Quill Edition

1 2 3 4 5 6 7 8 9 10

To Wendy

ACKNOWLEDGMENTS

Among those who have encouraged my frequent expoundings on trivia are Martin and Pamela Anisman, Roger and Tina Bergh, Rod and Sarah Lane, Rocco and Rae Orlando, Michael Adanti, and Bud Stone. My children are to be thanked for exhibiting sufficient interest and pride to inspire me to produce a sequel. Katharine Harris once again has been able to interpret my handwriting and type an error-free manuscript.

The staff of William Morrow and Company has been most helpful. Special thanks are owed to Cheryl Asherman, Harvey Hoffman, Bernard Schleifer and Veronica Windholz. Their remarkable talents have contributed significantly to a fine production. I am indebted to Jane Cavolina Meara who chose the work for the company and directed the project from start to finish. Her enthusiasm, encouragement, and suggestions have greatly improved the book.

The contributions of my wife, Wendy, to this book have been enormous. As ever I owe her so much.

—R.A.N.

CONTENTS

INTRODUCTION

The universal appeal of trivia is difficult to explain. Knowing the answers to trivia questions is not a sign of superior intelligence. Rather, it demonstrates that buffs have a high tolerance, even a craving, for the obscure and the forgotten. Why should so many individuals develop such passion for isolated facts?

One appeal is certainly nostalgia: bringing enjoyable or memorable experiences of the past into the present. Another is that most people are not earth shakers—their decisions do not noticeably affect the course of events; instead, they deal with routine and—to most everyone else—trivial items. For those who don't have answers to the problems of crime, war, hunger, disease, pollution, inflation, or unemployment, it's reassuring to know something definite.

The friends of trivia have varying degrees of commitment. Some concentrate their attention on a single area of information, such as sports, movies, Presidents, music, the Civil War. Others such as myself may feel at home with one or two areas but generally have more eclectic interests, enjoying a fact because of its uniqueness rather than its category. There are those who do extensive research to add to their store of facts; others are merely delighted when they meet some tidbit that they may or may not remember thereafter.

Like the first volume, *The New College of Trivial Knowledge* is written to appeal primarily to this latter group, although its preparation required being a member of the former. The questions in this book are intended to be "fair trivia": that is, questions that an average person might be able to answer merely because of his or her experience, background, and memory.

The New College of Trivial Knowledge consists of a series of factual tests on a variety of subjects, including: movies, sports, television, radio, literature, theatre, science, history, and art. Each test consists of three levels, the B. A., the M. S., and the Ph. D., reflecting increasing degrees of difficulty. Readers with different backgrounds may question my assignments to the various levels, but an honest attempt has been made to place the questions in the level that seems most appropriate.

Most of the tests are of the matching type, so readers can use a bit of the process of elimination in making their answers. Taking these tests can prove educational as well as entertaining. While all of the answers are provided at the end of the book, it's more fun if you complete the test before checking your results.

Good luck in becoming a spermologer (a collector of trivia)!

—R.A.N.

Test 1

Now Listen Up, Pilgrim—The Duke

John Wayne was a legend. He was also a better actor than many critics would admit. He usually played men larger than life. He loved and fought for many beautiful women in his films. Match Wayne's leading ladies with the movies in which they appeared as the Duke's love interest.

The B.A. Level

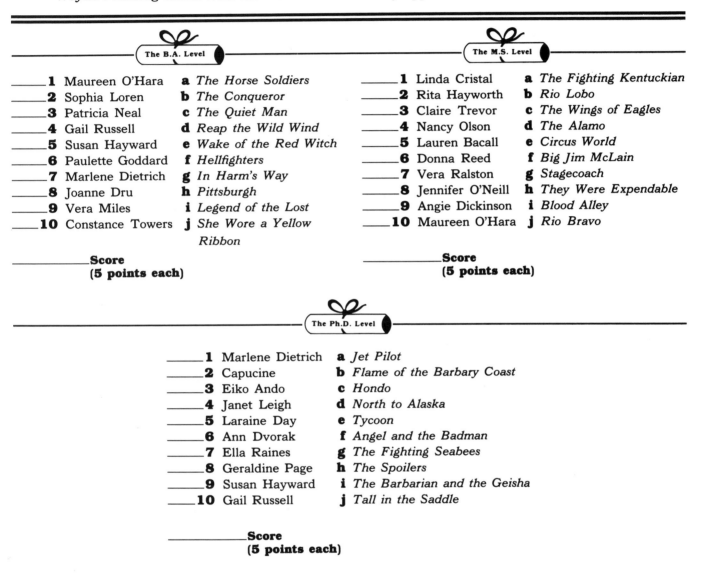

______**1** Maureen O'Hara	**a**	*The Horse Soldiers*
______**2** Sophia Loren	**b**	*The Conqueror*
______**3** Patricia Neal	**c**	*The Quiet Man*
______**4** Gail Russell	**d**	*Reap the Wild Wind*
______**5** Susan Hayward	**e**	*Wake of the Red Witch*
______**6** Paulette Goddard	**f**	*Hellfighters*
______**7** Marlene Dietrich	**g**	*In Harm's Way*
______**8** Joanne Dru	**h**	*Pittsburgh*
______**9** Vera Miles	**i**	*Legend of the Lost*
______**10** Constance Towers	**j**	*She Wore a Yellow Ribbon*

__________**Score**
(5 points each)

The M.S. Level

______**1** Linda Cristal	**a**	*The Fighting Kentuckian*
______**2** Rita Hayworth	**b**	*Rio Lobo*
______**3** Claire Trevor	**c**	*The Wings of Eagles*
______**4** Nancy Olson	**d**	*The Alamo*
______**5** Lauren Bacall	**e**	*Circus World*
______**6** Donna Reed	**f**	*Big Jim McLain*
______**7** Vera Ralston	**g**	*Stagecoach*
______**8** Jennifer O'Neill	**h**	*They Were Expendable*
______**9** Angie Dickinson	**i**	*Blood Alley*
______**10** Maureen O'Hara	**j**	*Rio Bravo*

__________**Score**
(5 points each)

The Ph.D. Level

______**1** Marlene Dietrich	**a**	*Jet Pilot*
______**2** Capucine	**b**	*Flame of the Barbary Coast*
______**3** Eiko Ando	**c**	*Hondo*
______**4** Janet Leigh	**d**	*North to Alaska*
______**5** Laraine Day	**e**	*Tycoon*
______**6** Ann Dvorak	**f**	*Angel and the Badman*
______**7** Ella Raines	**g**	*The Fighting Seabees*
______**8** Geraldine Page	**h**	*The Spoilers*
______**9** Susan Hayward	**i**	*The Barbarian and the Geisha*
______**10** Gail Russell	**j**	*Tall in the Saddle*

__________**Score**
(5 points each)

Test 2

And the Winner Is—Best Song

Many memorable songs have won Academy Awards for Best Song. In other years, however, the pickings were mighty slim. Match the Oscar-winning song with the movie in which it was featured.

The B.A. Level

_____**1** "Secret Love"
_____**2** "Chim Chim Cher-ee"
_____**3** "Over the Rainbow"
_____**4** "Evergreen"
_____**5** "Talk to the Animals"
_____**6** "Raindrops Keep Fallin' on My Head"
_____**7** "When You Wish Upon a Star"
_____**8** "White Christmas"
_____**9** "Sweet Leilani"
_____**10** "The Morning After"

a *A Star Is Born*
b *Butch Cassidy and the Sundance Kid*
c *Holiday Inn*
d *Mary Poppins*
e *The Wizard of Oz*
f *Waikiki Wedding*
g *Calamity Jane*
h *The Poseidon Adventure*
i *Pinocchio*
j *Doctor Doolittle*

__________**Score**
(5 points each)

The M.S. Level

_____**1** "Lullaby of Broadway"
_____**2** "On the Atchison, Topeka, and Sante Fe"
_____**3** "All the Way"
_____**4** "High Hopes"
_____**5** "Moon River"
_____**6** "I'm Easy"
_____**7** "We May Never Love Like This Again"
_____**8** "Thanks for the Memory"
_____**9** "Swinging on a Star"
_____**10** "It Might as Well Be Spring"

a *The Towering Inferno*
b *The Joker Is Wild*
c *Going My Way*
d *Nashville*
e *The Harvey Girls*
f *A Hole in the Head*
g *The Big Broadcast of 1938*
h *Breakfast at Tiffany's*
i *State Fair*
j *Gold Diggers of 1935*

__________**Score**
(5 points each)

The Ph.D. Level

_____**1** "Call Me Irresponsible"
_____**2** "Mona Lisa"
_____**3** "You'll Never Know"
_____**4** "For All We Know"
_____**5** "The Shadow of Your Smile"
_____**6** "Continental"
_____**7** "Baby It's Cold Outside"
_____**8** "The Last Time I Saw Paris"
_____**9** "The Way You Look Tonight"
_____**10** "In the Cool, Cool, Cool of the Evening"

a *The Sandpiper*
b *Papa's Delicate Condition*
c *Swingtime*
d *The Gay Divorcee*
e *Captain Carey, USA*
f *Lady Be Good*
g *Here Comes The Groom*
h *Neptune's Daughter*
i *Lovers and Other Strangers*
j *Hello, Frisco, Hello*

__________**Score**
(5 points each)

Test 3

Mr. President

How well do you know the Presidents of the United States? Identify the President from the clue given about him.

The B.A. Level

1.____________ The first President to die while in office.

2.____________ He was preceded and succeeded by the same man.

3.____________ The first American recipient of a Nobel Prize.

4.____________ The only President to resign from office.

5.____________ He was sworn into office by a woman.

6.____________ He never married.

7.____________ After serving as President he became a congressman.

8.____________ The only President who was a Roman Catholic.

9.____________ The only President who was divorced.

10.____________ First president to throw out a ball to begin the baseball season.

____________**Score**
(5 points each)

The M.S. Level

1.____________ First President born west of the Mississippi River.

2.____________ First President licensed to pilot an airplane.

3.____________ Never attended school; was taught to read at seventeen by his wife.

4.____________ The last surviving signer of the Constitution.

5.____________ First President born beyond the boundaries of the original thirteen states.

6.____________ Only President elected to office who was not renominated by his party for a second term.

7.____________ Only President to attain the thirty-third degree of the Masons.

8.____________ Before being elected President he had been an elected official less than three years.

9.____________ The only President sworn in by a former President.

10.____________ First President born a citizen of the United States.

____________**Score**
(5 points each)

The Ph.D. Level

1.____________ First "dark horse" elected President; not even mentioned on the first seven ballots of the convention that nominated him.

2.____________ First presidential candidate named by a national convention.

3.____________ The capital city of an African nation was named in his honor.

4.____________ Claimed he only knew two tunes; one was "Yankee Doodle" and the other wasn't.

5.____________ The first senator in office to be elected President.

6.____________ First defeated vice-presidential nominee elected president.

7.____________ First governor of a state to be elected President.

8.____________ Declined an honorary degree from Oxford because he did not have a classical education.

9.____________ First President who had not served in the U.S. Congress or the Continental Congress.

10.____________ A bachelor when elected President, he married his ward in the White House.

____________**Score**
(5 points each)

Test 4

The Play's the Thing—Shakespearean Characters

The influence of William Shakespeare on English-speaking people cannot be measured. This test is designed to determine if you recall characters from his plays. Warning: they are not always major characters. Match the characters with the plays in which they appeared.

The B.A. Level

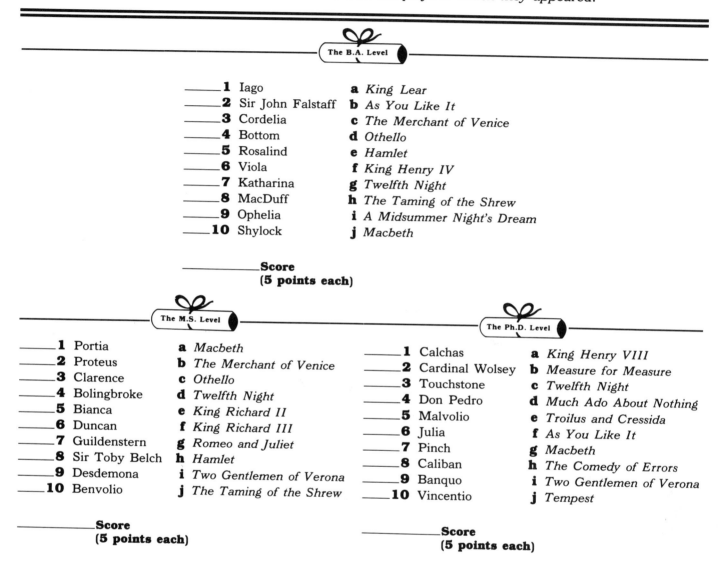

____ **1** Iago	**a** *King Lear*
____ **2** Sir John Falstaff	**b** *As You Like It*
____ **3** Cordelia	**c** *The Merchant of Venice*
____ **4** Bottom	**d** *Othello*
____ **5** Rosalind	**e** *Hamlet*
____ **6** Viola	**f** *King Henry IV*
____ **7** Katharina	**g** *Twelfth Night*
____ **8** MacDuff	**h** *The Taming of the Shrew*
____ **9** Ophelia	**i** *A Midsummer Night's Dream*
____ **10** Shylock	**j** *Macbeth*

____ **Score (5 points each)**

The M.S. Level

____ **1** Portia	**a** *Macbeth*
____ **2** Proteus	**b** *The Merchant of Venice*
____ **3** Clarence	**c** *Othello*
____ **4** Bolingbroke	**d** *Twelfth Night*
____ **5** Bianca	**e** *King Richard II*
____ **6** Duncan	**f** *King Richard III*
____ **7** Guildenstern	**g** *Romeo and Juliet*
____ **8** Sir Toby Belch	**h** *Hamlet*
____ **9** Desdemona	**i** *Two Gentlemen of Verona*
____ **10** Benvolio	**j** *The Taming of the Shrew*

____ **Score (5 points each)**

The Ph.D. Level

____ **1** Calchas	**a** *King Henry VIII*
____ **2** Cardinal Wolsey	**b** *Measure for Measure*
____ **3** Touchstone	**c** *Twelfth Night*
____ **4** Don Pedro	**d** *Much Ado About Nothing*
____ **5** Malvolio	**e** *Troilus and Cressida*
____ **6** Julia	**f** *As You Like It*
____ **7** Pinch	**g** *Macbeth*
____ **8** Caliban	**h** *The Comedy of Errors*
____ **9** Banquo	**i** *Two Gentlemen of Verona*
____ **10** Vincentio	**j** *Tempest*

____ **Score (5 points each)**

Test 5

Potpourri—Miscellaneous Trivia

The B.A. Level

1.____________________ What was the name of Pinocchio's creator and "father"?

2.____________________ What was the name of Eleanor Roosevelt's newspaper column?

3.____________________ The book *Silent Spring* has what for its main theme?

4.____________________ What breed of horses pull the Budweiser beer wagon?

5.____________________ Who was the evil overseer and slave-driver in *Uncle Tom's Cabin*?

6.____________________ Who was the sponsor of *Your Hit Parade* on radio?

7.____________________ Whose portrait appears on a $100 bill.

8.____________________ In what story is Christopher Robin a character?

9.____________________ Who played Alexander Waverly, head of policy and operations for U.N.C.L.E.?

10.____________________ Who is the voice of Porky Pig?

__________**Score**
(5 points each)

The M.S. Level

1.____________________ Who is the green-skinned Dr. Seuss character who steals Christmas?

2.____________________ What is the name of Thomas Jefferson's home in Virginia?

3.____________________ Who developed the process of vaccination?

4.____________________ How did Socrates commit suicide?

5.____________________ *Present Indicative* is the autobiography of which playwright?

6.____________________ Who was the Russian spy exchanged for U-2 pilot Gary Powers?

7.____________________ Who founded the American Red Cross Society?

8.____________________ What was the name of Robert Fulton's steamboat?

9.____________________ What is the name of Scrooge's dead partner?

10.____________________ Who is the basketball coach at the University of Notre Dame?

__________**Score**
(5 points each)

The Ph.D. Level

1.____________________ Who is the patron saint of Scotland?

2.____________________ What is the motto of the Rotary Club?

3.____________________ What was the name of Dorothy's uncle in *The Wizard of Oz*?

4.____________________ Who invented the pendulum clock?

5.____________________ Who wrote the Uncle Remus stories?

6.____________________ What is an elegy?

7.____________________ In what Dostoevski novel is the student Raskolnikov the protagonist?

8.____________________ What was the last album the Beatles recorded together?

9.____________________ What is the date of Bastille Day?

10.____________________ Who were Chang and Eng?

__________**Score**
(5 points each)

Test 6

The Russians Are Coming

The relationship of the United States with the U.S.S.R. has never been better than peaceful distrust. Politicians are elected (and defeated) by alternatively arguing that we should be tough or friendly with the Russians. Each of the following men and women of Russian extraction should be identifiable from the brief clue given.

The B.A. Level

_____ **1** Yuri Gagarin
_____ **2** Ivan the Terrible
_____ **3** Rudolf Nureyev
_____ **4** Aleksandr I. Solzhenitsyn
_____ **5** Boris Pasternak
_____ **6** Rasputin
_____ **7** Leonid Brezhnev
_____ **8** Anton Chekhov
_____ **9** Vladimir Horowitz
_____ **10** Sergei Prokofiev

a defector, made ballet history teaming with Margot Fonteyn
b dramatist; plays include *The Seagull* and *The Three Sisters*
c from 1964 until his death, First Secretary of the Communist Party
d compelled by the Russian government to decline Nobel Prize
e first man to orbit in space
f concert pianist; famous for his mastery of technique
g novelist; books chiefly based on his experience in Soviet labor camps
h composer of *Peter and the Wolf*
i first to assume title of Czar
j monk who gained great influence over the royal family

_____ **Score (5 points each)**

The M.S. Level

_____ **1** Vyacheslav Molotov
_____ **2** Vladimir Nabokov
_____ **3** Sol Hurok
_____ **4** Sergei Eisenstein
_____ **5** Alexander Borodin
_____ **6** Boris Spassky
_____ **7** Yevgeny Yevtushenko
_____ **8** Georgi Malenkov
_____ **9** Vaslav Nijinsky
_____ **10** Aram Khachaturian

a Soviet chess master; defeated by Bobby Fischer
b poet; criticized by his government for breaking from socialist realism
c had an explosive "cocktail" named after him
d foremost male ballet dancer of his time
e succeeded Stalin as premier
f composer, best known for unfinished opera *Prince Igor*
g film director; pictures include *Ten Days That Shook the World*
h composer; best known for his Gayne Ballet
i American impresario; brought famous European companies to U.S.
j novelist; works include *Pale Fire* and *The Gift*

_____ **Score (5 points each)**

The Ph.D. Level

_____ **1** Nicholas II
_____ **2** Peter the Great
_____ **3** Feodor Chaliapin
_____ **4** Alla Nazimova
_____ **5** Sergei Diaghilev
_____ **6** Marc Chagall
_____ **7** Andrei Gromyko
_____ **8** Dimitri Mendeleyev
_____ **9** Alexander Kerensky
_____ **10** Wassily Kandinsky

a painter; with Klee and others founded Abstract Expressionism
b the last czar; forced to abdicate, executed with his family
c chemist; discovered the periodic law
d opera singer; famous for interpretation of *Boris Godunov*
e statesman; once Soviet ambassador to Washington and chief delegate to the United Nations
f founder of the Ballet Russe
g stage and screen actress; famous for portrayal of Ibsen heroines
h prime minister after first Russian revolution
i sought to end medieval social conditions in Russia
j painter; known for decorative theater panels, stained-glass windows, and biblical drawings

_____ **Score (5 points each)**

Test 7

And Then I Wrote—Authors

The works included in this test are not all necessarily among the hundred best ever written, but they and their authors should be familiar. Match the author with his or her work.

The B.A. Level

______**1** *You Can't Go Home Again*	**a** John Bunyan
______**2** *The Legend of Sleepy Hollow*	**b** Johannes Spyri
______**3** *The Great Gatsby*	**c** Frederick Lewis Allen
______**4** *Decline and Fall of the Roman Empire*	**d** Niccolo Machiavelli
______**5** *Only Yesterday*	**e** F. Scott Fitzgerald
______**6** *Heidi*	**f** Washington Irving
______**7** *The Robe*	**g** Clarence Day
______**8** *The Prince*	**h** Thomas Wolfe
______**9** *Life With Father*	**i** Edward Gibbon
______**10** *Pilgrim's Progress*	**j** Lloyd C. Douglas

__________**Score**
(5 points each)

The M.S. Level

______**1** *Outline of History*	**a** Nordhoff and Hall
______**2** *John Brown's Body*	**b** Immanuel Kant
______**3** *Critique of Pure Reason*	**c** Thomas A. Kempis
______**4** *Silent Spring*	**d** Gore Vidal
______**5** *Mayor of Casterbridge*	**e** Stephen Vincent Benet
______**6** *Mutiny on the Bounty*	**f** Mikhail Sholokov
______**7** *Hans Brinker*	**g** Mary Mapes Dodge
______**8** *Imitation of Christ*	**h** H. G. Wells
______**9** *Harvest on the Don*	**i** Rachel Carson
______**10** *Julian*	**j** Thomas Hardy

__________**Score**
(5 points each)

The Ph.D. Level

______**1** *Age of Innocence*	**a** Franz Kafka
______**2** *A Passage to India*	**b** Will Durant
______**3** *Theory of the Leisure Class*	**c** Robert S. Lynd
______**4** *Five Little Peppers and How They Grew*	**d** E. M. Forster
______**5** *Middletown*	**e** Margaret Sidney
______**6** *The Trial*	**f** Edith Wharton
______**7** *Up from the Ape*	**g** Thorsten Veblen
______**8** *Liliom*	**h** K. B. Gilden
______**9** *Hurry Sundown*	**i** Ernest Hooton
______**10** *Story of Philosophy*	**j** Franz Molnar

__________**Score**
(5 points each)

Test 8

And Then I Sang—Male Artists

Music fills our days. We hear it from radio, television, and movies. This test deals with pop music and the male singers who are most associated with the records that were hits. Match the singer with the song.

The B.A. Level

____**1** "It's Not Unusual"
____**2** "Crocodile Rock"
____**3** "Seasons in the Sun"
____**4** "Sunshine on My Shoulders"
____**5** "Jailhouse Rock"
____**6** "Don't Think Twice, It's All Right"
____**7** "There Goes My Everything"
____**8** "Cracklin' Rose"
____**9** "Happy Birthday, Sweet Sixteen"
____**10** "I Guess the Lord Must Be in New York City"
____**11** "Sail Away"
____**12** "Fire and Rain"

a Bob Dylan
b John Denver
c Neil Diamond
d Harry Nilsson
e Terry Jacks
f Neil Sedaka
g Tom Jones
h James Taylor
i Engelbert Humperdinck
j Randy Newman
k Elton John
l Elvis Presley

________**Score**
(5 points each)

The M.S. Level

____**1** "Peggy Sue"
____**2** "Catch a Falling Star"
____**3** "Clair"
____**4** "Kaw-Liga"
____**5** "Splish Splash"
____**6** "A Teenager's Romance"
____**7** "Waist Deep in the Big Muddy"
____**8** "It's Not for Me to Say"
____**9** "Love and Marriage"
____**10** "You Send Me"
____**11** "Great Balls of Fire"
____**12** "Time in a Bottle"

a Pete Seeger
b Bobby Darin
c Jim Croce
d Buddy Holly
e Frank Sinatra
f Jerry Lee Lewis
g Sam Cooke
h Gilbert O'Sullivan
i Perry Como
j Johnny Mathis
k Hank Williams
l Ricky Nelson

________**Score**
(5 points each)

The Ph.D. Level

____**1** "Sweet Soul Music"
____**2** "I Can't Stop Loving You"
____**3** "You're Breaking My Heart"
____**4** "Riders in the Sky"
____**5** "Return to Me"
____**6** "Ain't It a Shame"
____**7** "Go Away, Little Girl"
____**8** "Rags to Riches"
____**9** "Answer Me, My Love"
____**10** "I Apologize"
____**11** "The Cry of the Wild Goose"
____**12** "Wish You Were Here"

a Vic Damone
b Vaughn Monroe
c Frankie Laine
d Steve Lawrence
e Eddie Fisher
f Ray Charles
g Nat King Cole
h Dean Martin
i Billy Eckstine
j Otis Redding
k Tony Bennett
l Pat Boone

________**Score**
(5 points each)

And Then I Sang—Female Artists

Now we turn our attention to the ladies. Once again, you are asked to match the singer with the song.

The B.A. Level

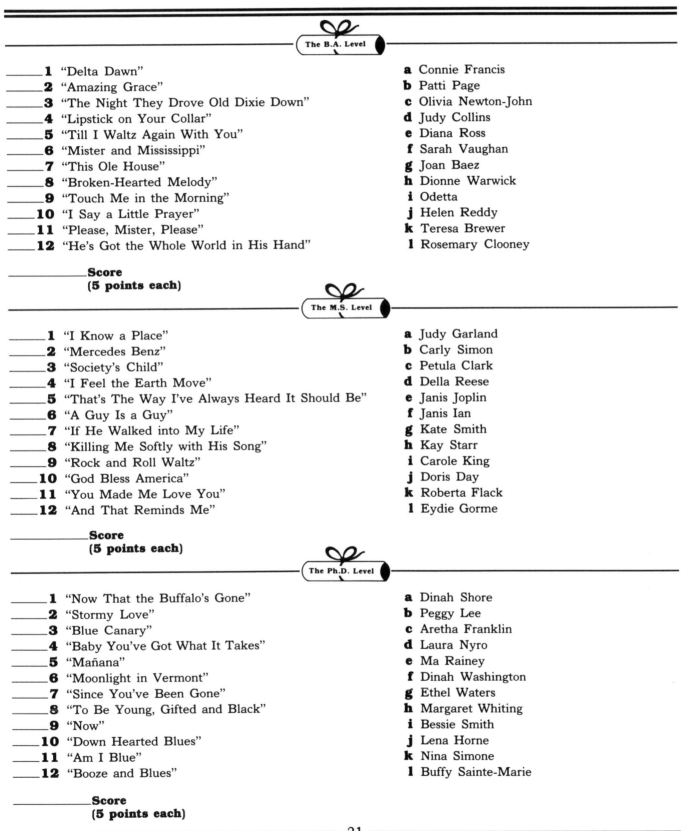

_____ **1** "Delta Dawn"
_____ **2** "Amazing Grace"
_____ **3** "The Night They Drove Old Dixie Down"
_____ **4** "Lipstick on Your Collar"
_____ **5** "Till I Waltz Again With You"
_____ **6** "Mister and Mississippi"
_____ **7** "This Ole House"
_____ **8** "Broken-Hearted Melody"
_____ **9** "Touch Me in the Morning"
_____ **10** "I Say a Little Prayer"
_____ **11** "Please, Mister, Please"
_____ **12** "He's Got the Whole World in His Hand"

a Connie Francis
b Patti Page
c Olivia Newton-John
d Judy Collins
e Diana Ross
f Sarah Vaughan
g Joan Baez
h Dionne Warwick
i Odetta
j Helen Reddy
k Teresa Brewer
l Rosemary Clooney

__________ **Score**
(5 points each)

The M.S. Level

_____ **1** "I Know a Place"
_____ **2** "Mercedes Benz"
_____ **3** "Society's Child"
_____ **4** "I Feel the Earth Move"
_____ **5** "That's The Way I've Always Heard It Should Be"
_____ **6** "A Guy Is a Guy"
_____ **7** "If He Walked into My Life"
_____ **8** "Killing Me Softly with His Song"
_____ **9** "Rock and Roll Waltz"
_____ **10** "God Bless America"
_____ **11** "You Made Me Love You"
_____ **12** "And That Reminds Me"

a Judy Garland
b Carly Simon
c Petula Clark
d Della Reese
e Janis Joplin
f Janis Ian
g Kate Smith
h Kay Starr
i Carole King
j Doris Day
k Roberta Flack
l Eydie Gorme

__________ **Score**
(5 points each)

The Ph.D. Level

_____ **1** "Now That the Buffalo's Gone"
_____ **2** "Stormy Love"
_____ **3** "Blue Canary"
_____ **4** "Baby You've Got What It Takes"
_____ **5** "Mañana"
_____ **6** "Moonlight in Vermont"
_____ **7** "Since You've Been Gone"
_____ **8** "To Be Young, Gifted and Black"
_____ **9** "Now"
_____ **10** "Down Hearted Blues"
_____ **11** "Am I Blue"
_____ **12** "Booze and Blues"

a Dinah Shore
b Peggy Lee
c Aretha Franklin
d Laura Nyro
e Ma Rainey
f Dinah Washington
g Ethel Waters
h Margaret Whiting
i Bessie Smith
j Lena Horne
k Nina Simone
l Buffy Sainte-Marie

__________ **Score**
(5 points each)

Test 10

Miscellaneous Sports Trivia

The B.A. Level

1.__________________ Who played George Gipp in the movie *Knute Rockne*?

2.__________________ What is the nickname of the Los Angeles hockey team?

3.__________________ Alvan Adams was the rookie-of-the-year in the NBA in 1975–76. For what team did he play?

4.__________________ Who was called the "Clown Prince of Basketball"?

5.__________________ Who played Ben Hogan in the movie *Follow the Sun?*

6.__________________ For what team did Tinkers, Evers, and Chance play together?

7.__________________ What position did Bill Mazeroski play with the Pittsburgh Pirates?

8.__________________ What is a grand slammer?

9.__________________ What is the score of a forfeited baseball game?

10.__________________ How many medals did the U.S. win in the 1980 summer Olympics?

__________**Score**
(5 points each)

The M.S. Level

1.__________________ What team did Nelson Fox star for?

2.__________________ What position did Hall of Famer Eddie Mathews play?

3.__________________ What former home-run king is a play-by-play announcer for the New York Mets?

4.__________________ What is the distance from the free throw line to the basket?

5.__________________ Who defeated Max Schmeling for the heavyweight championship?

6.__________________ Who is the only player to have appeared on three World Cup championship teams?

7.__________________ In golf, what is the number 1 wood club called?

8.__________________ What are the duties of a safety man in football?

9.__________________ What group awards the Heisman Trophy?

10.__________________ What year did Peggy Fleming win a gold medal for figure skating in the Olympics?

__________**Score**
(5 points each)

The Ph.D. Level

1.__________________ What is the name of Ted Williams's autobiography?

2.__________________ Which horse was named Harness Horse of the Year, three years in a row, 1964–66?

3.__________________ Which country has won the most Olympic gold medals in weightlifting?

4.__________________ Who was the last pitcher to legally throw a spitball?

5.__________________ Who played more games at shortstop than any other player?

6.__________________ Which coach invented the single wingback and double wingback formations?

7.__________________ Which player holds the NHL hockey record for scoring the most goals (53) as a rookie?

8.__________________ Who was the rookie-of-the-year in the NHL in 1972–73?

9.__________________ Who did Roberto Duran win the lightweight championship from?

10.__________________ Where did Carol "The Blaze" Blazejowski play college basketball?

__________**Score**
(5 points each)

Test 11

The Comics—What a Laugh

The comics are often the soap operas of the newspapers. They are not always funny but many have held our attention for decades. Others are topical, political, metaphysical. The best seem to speak some simple truths to their readers. Match the authors with their creations.

The B.A. Level

____ **1** "Andy Capp"	**a** Mik
____ **2** "Woody Woodpecker"	**b** Robert Ripley
____ **3** "Mighty Mouse"	**c** Walter Lantz
____ **4** "Ferd'nand"	**d** Marge
____ **5** "Hazel"	**e** Rube Goldberg
____ **6** "Believe It or Not"	**f** Paul Terry
____ **7** "Boob McNutt"	**g** Smythe
____ **8** "Hagar the Horrible"	**h** George McManus
____ **9** "Bringing Up Father"	**i** Ted Key
____ **10** "Little Lulu"	**j** Dik Browne

________ **Score**
(5 points each)

The M.S. Level

____ **1** "Smilin' Jack"	**a** Lom K. Ryan
____ **2** "Little Iodine"	**b** Zack Mosley
____ **3** "Buz Sawyer"	**c** Bud Fisher
____ **4** "Big George"	**d** Ed Dodd
____ **5** "Tumbleweeds"	**e** Roy Crane
____ **6** "Prince Valiant"	**f** Jimmy Hatlo
____ **7** "Mutt and Jeff"	**g** Parker and Hunt
____ **8** "Wizard of Id"	**h** Virgil Patch
____ **9** "Miss Peach"	**i** Mell Lazarus
____ **10** "Mark Trail"	**j** Hal Foster

________ **Score**
(5 points each)

The Ph.D. Level

____ **1** "Mary Worth"	**a** R. F. Outcault
____ **2** "Buster Brown"	**b** Otto Soglow
____ **3** "Winnie Winkle"	**c** Allen Saunders
____ **4** "Henry"	**d** M. M. Branner
____ **5** "Casper Milquetoast"	**e** George Baker
____ **6** "Alphonse and Gaston"	**f** Alex Kotzky
____ **7** "Sad Sack"	**g** F. Opper
____ **8** "Krazy Kat"	**h** Carl Anderson
____ **9** "Apartment 3G"	**i** Clare Briggs
____ **10** "Little King"	**j** George Herriman

________ **Score**
(5 points each)

Test 12

Songs of the Sixties

The opening lines of a song are often more memorable than the title. A good trivia buff should be able to match the two, especially with these memorable songs of the sixties.

The B.A. Level

_____ **1** ". . ., picks up the rice in the church . . ."
_____ **2** "Is this the little girl I carried . . ."
_____ **3** "When the moon is in the seventh house . . ."
_____ **4** "Oh yeah, I'll tell you something . . ."
_____ **5** "If you see me walkin' down the street . . ."
_____ **6** "Once upon a time you dressed so fine . . ."
_____ **7** "Bows and flows of angel hair . . ."
_____ **8** "Once upon a time there was a tavern . . ."
_____ **9** "Oh, you can kiss me on a Monday . . ."
_____ **10** "It's knowing that your door is always open . . ."
_____ **11** "If it takes forever . . ."
_____ **12** "Tall and tan and young and lovely . . ."
_____ **13** "Would you like to ride in my beautiful balloon . . ."
_____ **14** "How many roads must a man walk down . . ."
_____ **15** "When you're alone and life is making you lonely . . ."

a "Gentle on My Mind"
b "Those Were the Days"
c "I Will Wait for You"
d "Like a Rolling Stone"
e "Both Sides Now"
f "Blowin' in the Wind"
g "Eleanor Rigby"
h "The Girl from Ipanema"
i "Up, Up and Away"
j "Aquarius"
k "Sunrise, Sunset"
l "Downtown"
m "I Want to Hold Your Hand"
n "Walk on By"
o "Never on Sunday"

_____ **Score**
(5 points each)

The M.S. Level

_____ **1** "When I was seventeen . . ."
_____ **2** "When hearts are passing in the night, in the lonely night . . ."
_____ **3** "Round like a circle in a spiral, like a wheel within a wheel . . ."
_____ **4** "I'm just mad about Saffron . . ."
_____ **5** "When you're weary, feelin' small . . ."
_____ **6** "It was the third of June, another sleepy, dusty, delta day . . ."
_____ **7** "Trailer for sale or rent . . ."
_____ **8** "All my bags are packed, I'm ready to go . . ."
_____ **9** "Hello darkness my old friend . . ."
_____ **10** "No use permitting some prophet of doom . . ."
_____ **11** "Winds may blow o'er the icy sea . . ."
_____ **12** "Sittin' in the morning sun, I'll be sittin' when the evenin' come . . ."
_____ **13** "A time to be born, a time to die . . ."
_____ **14** "You know that it would be untrue . . ."
_____ **15** "And now the end is near . . ."

a "Bridge Over Troubled Waters"
b "Leaving on a Jet Plane"
c "King of the Road"
d "Ode to Billy Joe"
e "Turn, Turn, Turn"
f "The Sound of Silence"
g "Cabaret"
h "A Taste of Honey"
i "The Windmills of Your Mind"
j "A Man and a Woman"
k "Light My Fire"
l "My Way"
m "It Was a Very Good Year"
n "The Dock of the Bay"
o "Mellow Yellow"

_____ **Score**
(5 points each)

Test 12

The Ph.D. Level

_____ **1** "I remember when I was a very little girl . . ."
_____ **2** "What goes up must come down . . ."
_____ **3** "You never close your eyes anymore when I kiss your lips . . ."
_____ **4** "Show me the prison, show me the jail . . ."
_____ **5** "It's a still life watercolor of a now late afternoon . . ."
_____ **6** "I met a gin-soaked barroom queen in Memphis . . ."
_____ **7** "It was back in nineteen forty-two, I was a member of a good platoon . . ."
_____ **8** "Carnivals and cotton candy, carousels and calliopes . . ."
_____ **9** "We starve, look at one another short of breath . . ."
_____ **10** "Love is but the song we sing and fear's the way we die . . ."
_____ **11** "What you want, baby, I got . . ."
_____ **12** "Come to my door, baby . . ."
_____ **13** "Come gather 'round people wherever you roam . . ."
_____ **14** "It's a lesson too late for the learning . . ."
_____ **15** "I pulled into Nazareth, was feeling 'bout half past dead . . ."

a "Honky Tonk Woman"
b "You've Lost That Lovin' Feelin'"
c "Respect"
d "La Valse a Mille Temps"
e "Spinning Wheel"
f "Get Together"
g "Let the Sunshine In"
h "The Dangling Conversation"
i "The Weight"
j "Is That All There Is?"
k "Waist Deep in the Big Muddy"
l "The Last Thing on My Mind"
m "There But for Fortune"
n "Society's Child"
o "The Times They Are Changin'"

__________ **Score**
(5 points each)

Test 13

Memorable Movie Characters

You remember the movie, you remember the stars, but what were the names of the characters? Some names such as Rick Blaine, played by Humphrey Bogart in Casablanca, *stick with us. In this test, the characters should be so memorable that you can easily match them with the actor or actress who played them. To make things easier, you are given the movie in which the character appeared.*

The B.A. Level

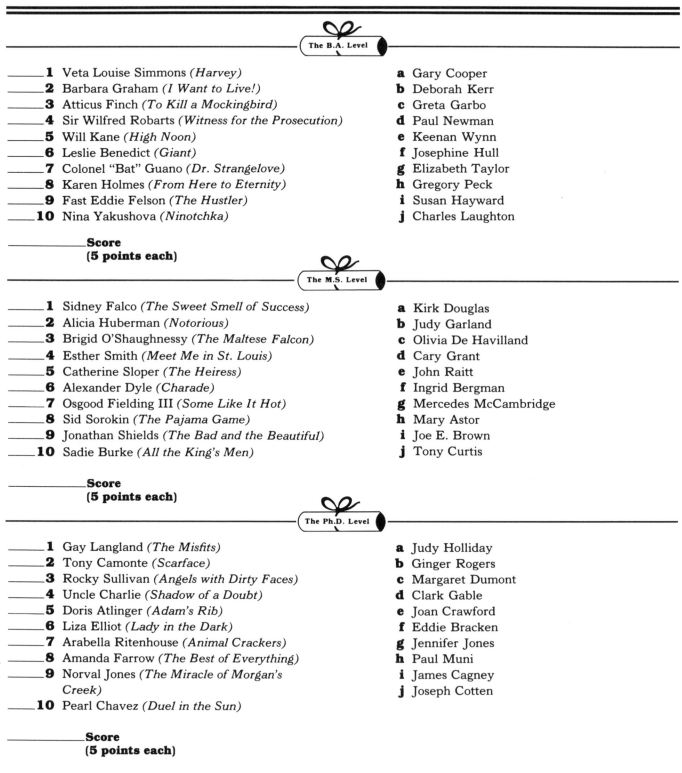

____ **1** Veta Louise Simmons *(Harvey)*	**a** Gary Cooper
____ **2** Barbara Graham *(I Want to Live!)*	**b** Deborah Kerr
____ **3** Atticus Finch *(To Kill a Mockingbird)*	**c** Greta Garbo
____ **4** Sir Wilfred Robarts *(Witness for the Prosecution)*	**d** Paul Newman
____ **5** Will Kane *(High Noon)*	**e** Keenan Wynn
____ **6** Leslie Benedict *(Giant)*	**f** Josephine Hull
____ **7** Colonel "Bat" Guano *(Dr. Strangelove)*	**g** Elizabeth Taylor
____ **8** Karen Holmes *(From Here to Eternity)*	**h** Gregory Peck
____ **9** Fast Eddie Felson *(The Hustler)*	**i** Susan Hayward
____ **10** Nina Yakushova *(Ninotchka)*	**j** Charles Laughton

________ **Score**
(5 points each)

The M.S. Level

____ **1** Sidney Falco *(The Sweet Smell of Success)*	**a** Kirk Douglas
____ **2** Alicia Huberman *(Notorious)*	**b** Judy Garland
____ **3** Brigid O'Shaughnessy *(The Maltese Falcon)*	**c** Olivia De Havilland
____ **4** Esther Smith *(Meet Me in St. Louis)*	**d** Cary Grant
____ **5** Catherine Sloper *(The Heiress)*	**e** John Raitt
____ **6** Alexander Dyle *(Charade)*	**f** Ingrid Bergman
____ **7** Osgood Fielding III *(Some Like It Hot)*	**g** Mercedes McCambridge
____ **8** Sid Sorokin *(The Pajama Game)*	**h** Mary Astor
____ **9** Jonathan Shields *(The Bad and the Beautiful)*	**i** Joe E. Brown
____ **10** Sadie Burke *(All the King's Men)*	**j** Tony Curtis

________ **Score**
(5 points each)

The Ph.D. Level

____ **1** Gay Langland *(The Misfits)*	**a** Judy Holliday
____ **2** Tony Camonte *(Scarface)*	**b** Ginger Rogers
____ **3** Rocky Sullivan *(Angels with Dirty Faces)*	**c** Margaret Dumont
____ **4** Uncle Charlie *(Shadow of a Doubt)*	**d** Clark Gable
____ **5** Doris Atlinger *(Adam's Rib)*	**e** Joan Crawford
____ **6** Liza Elliot *(Lady in the Dark)*	**f** Eddie Bracken
____ **7** Arabella Ritenhouse *(Animal Crackers)*	**g** Jennifer Jones
____ **8** Amanda Farrow *(The Best of Everything)*	**h** Paul Muni
____ **9** Norval Jones *(The Miracle of Morgan's Creek)*	**i** James Cagney
____ **10** Pearl Chavez *(Duel in the Sun)*	**j** Joseph Cotten

________ **Score**
(5 points each)

Test
14

Lights, Cameras, Action—The Directors

Many people, the author included, believe the real stars in the movies are the directors. After all, usually the actors spend a moment or two before the cameras with as many takes as the director feels necessary. The director must see the "whole picture" in a very real sense. Match the following wonderful movies with their creative directors.

The B.A. Level

______**1** *Hamlet*	**a** Cecil B. De Mille
______**2** *Blow Up*	**b** Vittorio De Sica
______**3** *Cabaret*	**c** Woody Allen
______**4** *Fort Apache*	**d** Laurence Olivier
______**5** *The Bicycle Thief*	**e** Vincente Minnelli
______**6** *Chinatown*	**f** Frank Capra
______**7** *Gigi*	**g** Bob Fosse
______**8** *The Greatest Show on Earth*	**h** John Ford
______**9** *Nashville*	**i** Michael Curtiz
______**10** *Casablanca*	**j** Michelangelo Antonioni
______**11** *It's a Wonderful Life*	**k** Roman Polanski
______**12** *Annie Hall*	**l** Robert Altman

__________**Score**
(5 points each)

The M.S. Level

______**1** *My Fair Lady*	**a** Francois Truffaut
______**2** *The Asphalt Jungle*	**b** Milos Forman
______**3** *Lolita*	**c** Charles Chaplin
______**4** *Exodus*	**d** John Huston
______**5** *Hello Dolly*	**e** Leo McCarey
______**6** *Monsieur Verdoux*	**f** Ingmar Bergman
______**7** *Fahrenheit 451*	**g** Paul Newman
______**8** *One Flew Over the Cuckoo's Nest*	**h** Joshua Logan
______**9** *Rachel, Rachel*	**i** Stanley Kubrick
______**10** *Picnic*	**j** Gene Kelly
______**11** *Cries and Whispers*	**k** Otto Preminger
______**12** *Going My Way*	**l** George Cukor

__________**Score**
(5 points each)

The Ph.D. Level

______**1** *The Desperate Hours*	**a** Billy Wilder
______**2** *Mr. Deeds Goes To Town*	**b** Robert Wise
______**3** *The Lost Weekend*	**c** Roberto Rossellini
______**4** *Gypsy*	**d** William Wellman
______**5** *The Sound of Music*	**e** Sidney Lumet
______**6** *Marty*	**f** Frank Capra
______**7** *A Place in the Sun*	**g** Mervyn LeRoy
______**8** *Two for the Road*	**h** Federico Fellini
______**9** *The Ox-Bow Incident*	**i** Delbert Mann
______**10** *Paisan*	**j** William Wyler
______**11** *Amarcord*	**k** Stanley Donen
______**12** *Network*	**l** George Stevens

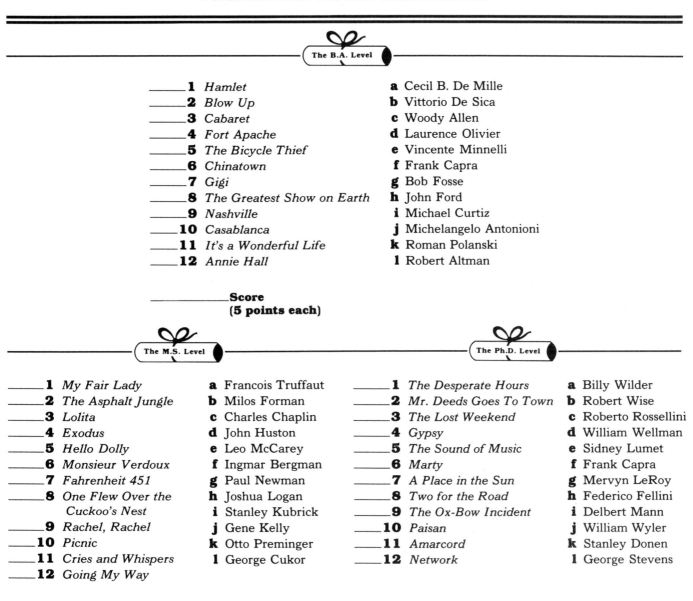

__________**Score**
(5 points each)

Test
15

Miscellaneous Movie Trivia

The B.A. Level

1.________________ What was the occupation of the title character in the movie *Marty?*

2.________________ What was the name of the James Dean character in *Giant?*

3.________________ Burt Lancaster was Wyatt Earp. Who played Doc Holliday?

4.________________ Liberace starred in only one movie. What was it?

5.________________ What was Paul Newman's first and probably worst film?

6.________________ Who played Judy Garland's little sister in *Meet Me in St. Louis?*

7.________________ Who was the "Wistful Widow of Wagon Gap" in the Abbott and Costello movie of that name?

8.________________ With what movie star do you associate a torn T-shirt?

9.________________ Name the two Oscar-winning sisters of the thirties and forties?

10.________________ Who was known as "the man of a thousand faces?"

__________**Score**
(5 points each)

The M.S. Level

1.________________ Who played Gilda's embittered and dangerous husband?

2.________________ Who was the narrator of *To Kill a Mockingbird?*

3.________________ Who was Spencer Tracy's unruly charge in *Boy's Town?*

4.________________ Which actor in *Cool Hand Luke* said, "What we have here is failure to communicate?"

5.________________ What picture was advertised with the slogan "Garbo Talks"?

6.________________ Who played the title role in the movie *Wilson?*

7.________________ What type of plane endangered Cary Grant in *North by Northwest?*

8.________________ Who played Dr. Livingstone in *Stanley and Livingstone?*

9.________________ What role did Boris Karloff play in *Tower of London?*

10.________________ What was the first Abbott and Costello movie to feature the Andrews sisters?

__________**Score**
(5 points each)

The Ph.D. Level

1.________________ Who played the genie in *The Thief of Bagdad?*

2.________________ Which actress was the Bride of Frankenstein?

3.________________ Which role did Leon Errol play in *Gentleman Joe Palooka?*

4.________________ Who played Little Beaver to William Elliott's Red Ryder?

5.________________ What was the real identity of Tarzan?

6.________________ In what Marx brothers movie did Louis Calhern appear as a villain?

7.________________ Who was David Niven's male traveling companion in *Around the World in Eighty Days?*

8.________________ Who was Cary Grant's new wife in *Arsenic and Old Lace?*

9.________________ Which actor played each of the historical personages: Hamilton, Rothschild, Richelieu, and Disraeli?

10.________________ What was the only movie made together by Al Jolson and his wife, Ruby Keeler?

__________**Score**
(5 points each)

Test 16

Remember the Sixties

The sixties were an exciting time, filled with names and events that will never be forgotten. Or will they? Answer the following questions and prove that you were impressed by the news of that decade.

The B.A. Level

1.____________________ What was the volunteer group created by executive order of President Kennedy to meet the urgent need of skilled manpower in underdeveloped countries?

2.____________________ Who was the Harvard professor who dropped out to become a proselytizer of the use of LSD?

3.____________________ Who received the Nobel Peace Prize for his leadership in the civil rights movement and his advocacy of nonviolence?

4.____________________ Pope Paul issued an encyclical reaffirming the Church's opposition to all forms of birth control except one. Which one?

5.____________________ What was the name of the book written by Norman Mailer that immortalized the anti-war demonstration at the Pentagon?

6.____________________ Despite his conviction for taking $250,000 in union funds, he was reelected to a five-year term as Teamster president. Name him.

7.____________________ Who was ready to fight with his fists but not the Vietnamese?

8.____________________ Who said the Beatles were more popular than Jesus?

9.____________________ Where did the Cuban refugees land in an unsuccessful attempt to "liberate" their country?

10.____________________ What was the name of the scandal involving hundreds of disk jockeys?

____________**Score**
(5 points each)

The M.S. Level

1.____________________ What incident led to the collapse of the Paris summit between Eisenhower and Khrushchev?

2.____________________ Who was the first black coach of a major professional sports team?

3.____________________ Who was the convicted kidnapper and rapist who was executed despite worldwide protests?

4.____________________ Which senator was censured for paying personal debts with campaign contributions?

5.____________________ Who became the fifth nuclear power, in October 1964?

6.____________________ What movie was voted the best ever made in a poll of 70 film critics from eleven countries?

7.____________________ What was the book written by Ralph Nader demanding new safety regulations for automobiles?

8.____________________ Which Supreme Court Justice resigned after it was revealed that he had received a fee from a man convicted of selling unregistered securities?

9.____________________ Who was the peace candidate for President in 1968 whose strong showing in primaries contributed to President Johnson's decision not to seek reelection?

10.____________________ What 1.6 million member group left the AFL-CIO in 1967?

____________**Score**
(5 points each)

Test 16

The Ph.D. Level

1.____________________ What San Francisco district was favored by the flower children?

2.____________________ Who killed eight student nurses in their Chicago dormitory room?

3.____________________ What was the name of the first privately owned satellite?

4.____________________ Whose election to the chairmanship of SNCC began a shift from civil rights to Black Power in the black movement?

5.____________________ Which black congressman was barred from taking his seat in the House because he supposedly misused travel funds?

6.____________________ What was the name of the intelligence ship captured by North Korea in 1968?

7.____________________ What painting by Rembrandt was bought by the New York Metropolitan Museum of Art for a then record $2.3 million?

8.____________________ Who was the first black student to be admitted to the University of Mississippi? It took a federal court order.

9.____________________ What was the major content of the 24th Amendment to the Constitution ratified in 1964?

10.____________________ Who was the first black cabinet member in the United States?

____________**Score**
(5 points each)

Test 17

Music, Music, Music

This test is designed to determine your knowledge of musical terms, given their simplest definitions. Play on!

The B.A. Level

1.__________________ performance of music made up at the moment.

2.__________________ an introductory section of a popular song.

3.__________________ a secret means of communication between slaves as they worked in the fields.

4.__________________ music intended for small groups performed in intimate surroundings.

5.__________________ an informal gathering of musicians playing on their own time just for the fun of it.

6.__________________ a simple song usually romantic in nature using the same melody for each stanza.

7.__________________ the main body or refrain of a song.

8.__________________ songs that recount passages from scriptures for lyrics.

9.__________________ familiar well-established popular or jazz tune.

10.__________________ a small instrumental group consisting of from 3 to 8 players.

__________**Score**
(5 points each)

The M.S. Level

1.__________________ a congregational song, words not taken directly from the Bible, sung in praise to God.

2.__________________ red-light district in New Orleans where jazz prospered.

3.__________________ refers to the speed of the underlying beat.

4.__________________ a square dance of five figures popular in the nineteenth century.

5.__________________ simultaneous sounding of two or more tones.

6.__________________ pertaining to the rites and services of a religious ceremony.

7.__________________ the placing of an accent on a normally weak beat or weak part of a beat.

8.__________________ a name given to a type of religious song of the American Negro.

9.__________________ the succession of simple tones varying in pitch and rhythm having a recognizable musical shape.

10.__________________ a player in a musical ensemble, as differentiated from the leader.

__________**Score**
(5 points each)

The Ph.D. Level

1.__________________ refers to the artificial wavering of a tone, rapidly recurring fluctuation of pitch.

2.__________________ a short pattern of sounds which are repeated and played by a soloist or group.

3.__________________ a persistently repeated melodic and/or rhythmic figure.

4.__________________ use of two or more rhythmic patterns played simultaneously.

5.__________________ lowers the pitch one half step.

6.__________________ a design in which one section of a musical selection recurs intermittently with contracting sections coming between each repetition.

7.__________________ a tone sustained below while harmonies change.

8.__________________ a transitional chord or rhythmic progression of indefinite duration used as a filler until the soloist is ready to start or continue.

9.__________________ refers to the tuning system found on the keyboard.

10.__________________ raises the pitch one half step.

__________**Score**
(5 points each)

Test 18

National Book Awards—The Best of the Best

Writing a book is a great kick, having it published is even better, selling many copies is a kind of recognition, but winning an award, especially the prestigious National Book Award—ah, that's recognition. Match the authors with their prize-winning works.

The B.A. Level

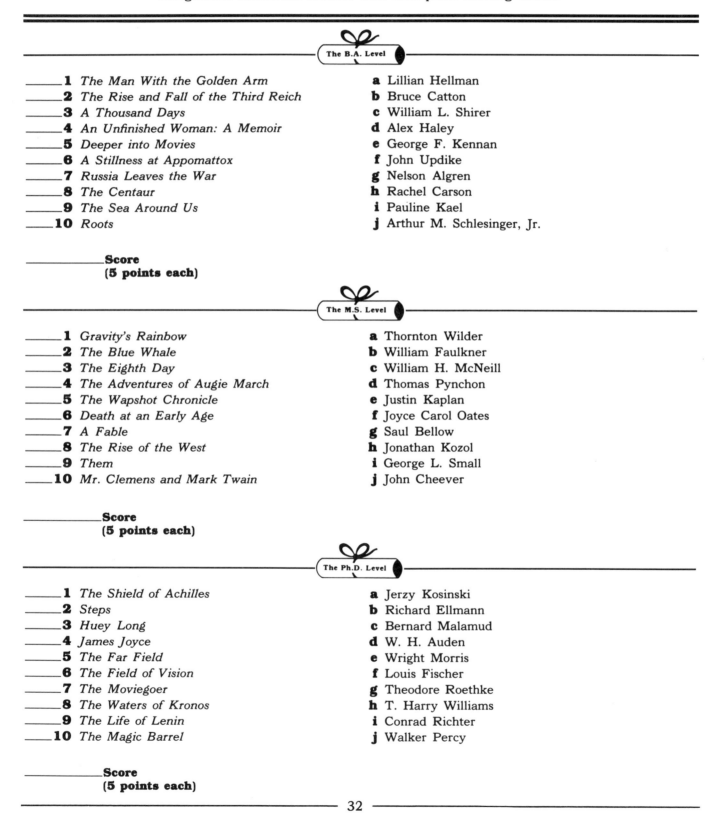

_____**1** *The Man With the Golden Arm*
_____**2** *The Rise and Fall of the Third Reich*
_____**3** *A Thousand Days*
_____**4** *An Unfinished Woman: A Memoir*
_____**5** *Deeper into Movies*
_____**6** *A Stillness at Appomattox*
_____**7** *Russia Leaves the War*
_____**8** *The Centaur*
_____**9** *The Sea Around Us*
_____**10** *Roots*

a Lillian Hellman
b Bruce Catton
c William L. Shirer
d Alex Haley
e George F. Kennan
f John Updike
g Nelson Algren
h Rachel Carson
i Pauline Kael
j Arthur M. Schlesinger, Jr.

__________**Score**
(5 points each)

The M.S. Level

_____**1** *Gravity's Rainbow*
_____**2** *The Blue Whale*
_____**3** *The Eighth Day*
_____**4** *The Adventures of Augie March*
_____**5** *The Wapshot Chronicle*
_____**6** *Death at an Early Age*
_____**7** *A Fable*
_____**8** *The Rise of the West*
_____**9** *Them*
_____**10** *Mr. Clemens and Mark Twain*

a Thornton Wilder
b William Faulkner
c William H. McNeill
d Thomas Pynchon
e Justin Kaplan
f Joyce Carol Oates
g Saul Bellow
h Jonathan Kozol
i George L. Small
j John Cheever

__________**Score**
(5 points each)

The Ph.D. Level

_____**1** *The Shield of Achilles*
_____**2** *Steps*
_____**3** *Huey Long*
_____**4** *James Joyce*
_____**5** *The Far Field*
_____**6** *The Field of Vision*
_____**7** *The Moviegoer*
_____**8** *The Waters of Kronos*
_____**9** *The Life of Lenin*
_____**10** *The Magic Barrel*

a Jerzy Kosinski
b Richard Ellmann
c Bernard Malamud
d W. H. Auden
e Wright Morris
f Louis Fischer
g Theodore Roethke
h T. Harry Williams
i Conrad Richter
j Walker Percy

__________**Score**
(5 points each)

Test 19

Hello There, Guv'nor

The governors of states are important men and women who lead their citizens for good or bad. Some are more famous, prominent, or infamous than others. You should have little difficulty in matching the following governors with the states of which they were chief executives.

The B.A. Level

____ **1**	Woodrow Wilson	**a**	Louisiana
____ **2**	Spiro T. Agnew	**b**	Minnesota
____ **3**	Huey P. Long, Jr.	**c**	New Jersey
____ **4**	Earl Warren	**d**	Texas
____ **5**	Lester G. Maddox	**e**	West Virginia
____ **6**	Harold E. Stassen	**f**	New York
____ **7**	Dixy Lee Ray	**g**	Maryland
____ **8**	John D. Rockefeller IV	**h**	Georgia
____ **9**	Thomas E. Dewey	**i**	California
____ **10**	John B. Connally	**j**	Washington

________ **Score**
(5 points each)

The M.S. Level

____ **1**	George W. Romney	**a**	Connecticut
____ **2**	Harold E. Hughes	**b**	Michigan
____ **3**	Abraham Ribicoff	**c**	Kansas
____ **4**	James E. Folsom	**d**	Pennsylvania
____ **5**	William W. Scranton	**e**	Iowa
____ **6**	Walter J. Hickel	**f**	Nevada
____ **7**	Terry Sanford	**g**	Alaska
____ **8**	Paul D. Laxalt	**h**	Alabama
____ **9**	Alfred M. Landon	**i**	Delaware
____ **10**	Pierre S. duPont	**j**	North Carolina

________ **Score**
(5 points each)

The Ph.D. Level

____ **1**	Theodore G. Bilbo	**a**	Arizona
____ **2**	James M. Curley	**b**	Tennessee
____ **3**	Frank G. Clement	**c**	South Carolina
____ **4**	Philip F. LaFollette	**d**	Kentucky
____ **5**	Otto Kerner	**e**	Mississippi
____ **6**	Orval E. Faubus	**f**	Massachusetts
____ **7**	Albert B. Chandler	**g**	Ohio
____ **8**	Michael V. DiSalle	**h**	Illinois
____ **9**	James F. Byrnes	**i**	Wisconsin
____ **10**	Paul J. Fannin	**j**	Arkansas

________ **Score**
(5 points each)

Test 20

More Potpourri

The B.A. Level

1.__________________ Where is the Country Music Hall of Fame located?

2.__________________ Which rubber manufacturer proudly announces "We're the guys without the blimp?"

3.__________________ Who was the host of the radio series *The Breakfast Club*?

4.__________________ What character is the personification of the British people?

5.__________________ What is the name of the rich boy in "Nancy" cartoons?

6.__________________ What was the name of the killer played by Humphrey Bogart in the movie *High Sierra*?

7.__________________ Who was the first host of *The Original Amateur Hour*?

8.__________________ Who wrote the book about her ex-profession, *A House Is Not a Home*?

9.__________________ The marriage of what U.S. citizen in Europe was covered by more than eighteen hundred members of the press in 1956?

10.__________________ Name the historical novel of gargantuan length written by Hervey Allen in the thirties?

__________**Score**
(5 points each)

The M.S. Level

1.__________________ What is the length of time of a U.S. patent?

2.__________________ What were the names of the two war-weary infantrymen created by Bill Mauldin?

3.__________________ What is the meaning of *ad hoc*?

4.__________________ What is a prime number?

5.__________________ Who was Hiawatha's wife in the Longfellow poem?

6.__________________ Who was the ringmaster of the TV series *Super Circus*?

7.__________________ Which character actor was Barry Fitzgerald's brother?

8.__________________ Who was the first Secretary of Health, Education and Welfare?

9.__________________ What rock opera created by The Who was later made into a movie?

10.__________________ Who is Ann Landers's twin sister?

__________**Score**
(5 points each)

The Ph.D. Level

1.__________________ What and where is Estoril?

2.__________________ What musical play was based on Shaw's *Arms and the Man*?

3.__________________ Who was the bystander who filmed the assassination of John F. Kennedy?

4.__________________ What is the name of the duck in Prokofiev's *Peter and the Wolf*?

5.__________________ Which was the first coeducational American college?

6.__________________ Name the author and his work about "the best of all possible worlds."

7.__________________ What is the occupation of the parents in *Cheaper by the Dozen*?

8.__________________ "Euclid alone has looked on Beauty bare" is a sonnet by whom?

9.__________________ The play *The Heiress* is an adaptation of which novel by Henry James?

10.__________________ Name the art of bookbinding.

__________**Score**
(5 points each)

Test 21

The Ladies, Bless Them—Barbara, Bette, and Joan

When the author was quite young, three magnificent actresses dominated movies. By today's standards they were not really beautiful, but they were talented. Salute Barbara Stanwyck, Bette Davis, and Joan Crawford by identifying their movies by the brief descriptions.

The B.A. Level

1.____________________ Travelers at a way station in the Arizona desert are held up by gangsters.

2.____________________ Stranded passengers in Pago Pago during an epidemic include a prostitute and a missionary.

3.____________________ An ambitious violinist gets emotionally involved with his wealthy patroness.

4.____________________ An insurance agent plans with the glamorous wife of a client to kill her husband.

5.____________________ A southern belle causes trouble because of her wilfulness and spite.

6.____________________ A revolutionary leader causes the downfall of Emperor Maximilian and his empress.

7.____________________ A crude, common woman embarrasses her blue-blood husband and smothers her daughter with mother-love.

8.____________________ The love life of Peggy O'Neal, protégée of Andrew Jackson.

9.____________________ The writer of a successful love and marriage column must make up a family for herself in the cause of publicity.

10.____________________ A poor boy is torn between two absorbing interests—prize fighting and the violin.

11.____________________ A tough carnival dancer is stranded in a small town and affects the lives of local politicians.

12.____________________ A well-to-do Englishman is brought down by his infatuation with a sluttish waitress.

__________**Score**
(5 points each)

The M.S. Level

1.____________________ A burlesque dancer solves a number of backstage murders.

2.____________________ A murderous child becomes a wealthy woman with a spineless husband.

3.____________________ A spinster starts a village school for Welsh minors and sees one enter Oxford.

4.____________________ A dowdy housewife leaves her husband, starts a restaurant chain, and survives a murder case.

5.____________________ A wife's only real love is her meticulously kept and richly appointed house.

6.____________________ A frustrated woman takes the psychiatric cure and embarks on a doomed love affair.

7.____________________ A family of schemers in post Civil War days will stop at nothing to outwit each other.

8.____________________ A woman gangster goes blind and falls in love with her doctor.

9.____________________ Three sisters refuse to sell their aristocratic mansion to make way for development.

10.____________________ A tramp is hired to embody the common man in a phony political drive and almost commits suicide.

11.____________________ An alcoholic actress is rehabilitated.

12.____________________ A fashion designer has two men in her life.

__________**Score**
(5 points each)

Test 21

The Ph.D. Level

1.____________________ A count arranges for a chorus girl to spend two weeks at an aristocratic resort, where she is pursued by two rich men.

2.____________________ A playwright heiress finds that her husband is plotting to kill her.

3.____________________ A lady cardsharp and her father are outsmarted on an ocean liner by a millionaire simpleton.

4.____________________ When her suitor is killed in the Civil War, an unmarried mother allows her childless cousin to raise her daughter as her own.

5.____________________ A good-time society girl discovers she is dying of a brain tumor.

6.____________________ A selfish beauty finally turns to her discarded dull husband when he is blind and her looks have faded.

7.____________________ A cattle baron feuds with his tempestuous daughter.

8.____________________ Seven professors compiling a dictionary give shelter to a stripteaser on the run from gangsters.

9.____________________ A woman deceives her husband by exchanging identities with her dead twin.

10.____________________ A blind Irish deaf mute girl is adopted by an American socialite and her plight becomes an international cause.

11.____________________ A psychopathic artist paints his wives as the Angel of Death, then murders them with poisoned milk.

12.____________________ A factory girl goes to New York in search of riches.

__________**Score**
(5 points each)

Test 22

Brush Up Your Shakespeare

The Bard has spoken and we have listened. The quotes in this test are well known. It won't be necessary for you to identify the characters who spoke the lines. Merely identify the plays in which they were delivered.

The B.A. Level

____ **1** "A horse! a horse! my kingdom for a horse."
____ **2** "The wish was father, Harry, to that thought."
____ **3** "All the world's a stage, and all the men and women merely players."
____ **4** "If music be the food of love, play on."
____ **5** "This above all: to thine own self be true."
____ **6** "The fault, dear Brutus, is not in our stars but in ourselves."
____ **7** "Out, damned spot! out, I say!"
____ **8** "Your daughter and the Moor are now making the beast with two backs."
____ **9** "Kiss me, Kate, we will be married o' Sunday."
____ **10** "Goodnight, goodnight! parting is such sweet sorrow."

a *Julius Caesar*
b *Macbeth*
c *Othello*
d *Hamlet*
e *Richard III*
f *The Taming of the Shrew*
g *Romeo and Juliet*
h *Henry IV*
i *As You Like It*
j *Twelfth Night*

________ **Score**
(5 points each)

The M.S. Level

____ **1** "O! that this too too solid flesh would melt."
____ **2** "Is this a dagger which I see before me?"
____ **3** "Lord, what fools these mortals be!"
____ **4** "But, soft! What light through yonder window breaks?"
____ **5** "This blessed plot, this earth, this realm, this England."
____ **6** "Once more unto the breach, dear friends, once more."
____ **7** "If you prick us, do we not bleed? if you tickle us, do we not laugh? if you poison us, do we not die? and if you wrong us, shall we not revenge?"
____ **8** "Be not afraid of greatness: some are born great, some achieve greatness, and some have greatness thrust upon them."
____ **9** "The better part of valor is discretion."
____ **10** "As he was valiant, I honor him; but as he was ambitious, I slew him."

a *Henry IV*
b *Richard II*
c *Hamlet*
d *Julius Caesar*
e *Twelfth Night*
f *The Merchant of Venice*
g *Romeo and Juliet*
h *Henry V*
i *Macbeth*
j *A Midsummer Night's Dream*

________ **Score**
(5 points each)

Test
22

The Ph.D. Level

_____ **1** "Who woo'd in haste and means to wed at leisure."
_____ **2** "Speak low, if you speak love."
_____ **3** "Who steals my purse steals trash."
_____ **4** "How sharper than a serpent's tooth it is to have a thankless child!"
_____ **5** "It is a wise father that knows his own son."
_____ **6** "I have more flesh than another man and therefore more frailty."
_____ **7** "The evil men do lives after them, the good is oft interred with their bones."
_____ **8** "My salad days when I was green in judgment."
_____ **9** "The first thing we do, let's kill all the lawyers."
_____ **10** "There's place and means for every man alive."

a *King Lear*
b *Antony and Cleopatra*
c *Much Ado About Nothing*
d *All's Well That Ends Well*
e *Julius Caesar*
f *The Taming of the Shrew*
g *Henry VI*
h *Othello*
i *The Merchant of Venice*
j *Henry IV*

__________ **Score**
(5 points each)

Test
23

Athletes of the Year

Sports editors of Associated Press-member newspapers annually select the male and female athlete-of-the-year from both professional and amateur ranks. This test is a piece of cake. Just name the sport for which the athlete is known.

The B.A. Level

1.____________ Mark Spitz
2.____________ Peggy Fleming
3.____________ Babe Didrikson Zaharias
4.____________ Nadia Comaneci
5.____________ Joe Louis
6.____________ Pepper Martin
7.____________ Jesse Owens
8.____________ Glenn Davis
9.____________ Maureen Connally
10.____________ Wilma Rudolph

__________**Score**
(5 points each)

The M.S. Level

1.____________ Patty Berg
2.____________ Helen Wills Moody
3.____________ Lou Boudreau
4.____________ Dawn Fraser
5.____________ Tommy Harmon
6.____________ Bryon Nelson
7.____________ Olga Korbut
8.____________ Ingemar Johansson
9.____________ Mickey Wright
10.____________ Steve Cauthen

__________**Score**
(5 points each)

The Ph.D. Level

1.____________ Rafer Johnson
2.____________ Pat McCormick
3.____________ Don Schollander
4.____________ Helen Jacobs
5.____________ Helen Stephens
6.____________ Don Budge
7.____________ Virginia Van Wie
8.____________ Gunder Haegg
9.____________ Gene Sarazen
10.____________ Helene Madison

__________**Score**
(5 points each)

Test 24

The Emmy Winners

The Emmy Award is presented annually for outstanding programs, performers, and behind-the-scenes talent in television broadcasting as well as for exceptional service or contribution to the industry. This test requires you to match a performer with his or her award-winning show.

The B.A. Level

_____ **1** Carl Betz	**a** ABC's *Wide World of Sports*
_____ **2** Cicely Tyson	**b** *Victoria Regina*
_____ **3** Jim McKay	**c** *The Andy Griffith Show*
_____ **4** Phil Silvers	**d** *Judd for the Defense*
_____ **5** Rod Serling	**e** *Upstairs, Downstairs*
_____ **6** Julie Harris	**f** *Macbeth*
_____ **7** William Holden	**g** *Twilight Zone*
_____ **8** Jean Marsh	**h** *The Blue Knight*
_____ **9** Judith Anderson	**i** *The Autobiography of Miss Jane Pittman*
_____ **10** Don Knotts	**j** *You'll Never Get Rich*

_________ **Score**
(5 points each)

The M.S. Level

_____ **1** Robert Cummings	**a** *Babe*
_____ **2** Alfred Lunt	**b** *Requiem for a Heavyweight*
_____ **3** Patty Duke	**c** *Harry S. Truman: Plain Speaking*
_____ **4** Susan Clark	**d** *A Christmas Memory*
_____ **5** Ed Flanders	**e** *On the Road*
_____ **6** Diana Hyland	**f** *The Magnificent Yankee*
_____ **7** Charles Kuralt	**g** *Twelve Angry Men*
_____ **8** Geraldine Page	**h** *Helen Morgan Story*
_____ **9** Polly Bergen	**i** *The Boy in the Plastic Bubble*
_____ **10** Jack Palance	**j** *My Sweet Charlie*

_________ **Score**
(5 points each)

The Ph.D. Level

_____ **1** Trevor Howard	**a** *Among the Paths to Eden*
_____ **2** Peter Ustinov	**b** *The Invincible Mr. Disraeli*
_____ **3** Susan Hampshire	**c** *Barefoot in Athens*
_____ **4** Anthony Hopkins	**d** *The Glass Menagerie*
_____ **5** Christopher Plummer	**e** *Male of the Species*
_____ **6** Burgess Meredith	**f** *Vanity Fair*
_____ **7** Paul Scofield	**g** *Tail Gunner Joe*
_____ **8** Maureen Stapleton	**h** *A Small Rebellion*
_____ **9** Simone Signoret	**i** *The Lindbergh Kidnapping*
_____ **10** Michael Moriarty	**j** *The Moneychangers*

_________ **Score**
(5 points each)

Test 25

Miscellaneous Sports Trivia

The B.A. Level

1.____________________ Who are the only two major league baseball players to receive more than 2,000 bases on balls in their careers?

2.____________________ What is the soccer term for hooking or kicking the ball away from an opponent?

3.____________________ Which side of the offensive line is referred to as the weak side?

4.____________________ Who was the originator of the face mask now worn by all NHL goal tenders?

5.____________________ What boxing title did Nino Benvenuti hold?

6.____________________ What weight must all horses carry in the Triple Crown races?

7.____________________ Who is third on the all-time home run list behind Aaron and Ruth?

8.____________________ What baseball player was nicknamed "The Yankee Clipper?"

9.____________________ In marking a baseball score card, what does a "K" stand for?

10.____________________ Where did the New York Mets play their games before moving to Shea Stadium?

__________**Score**
(5 points each)

The M.S. Level

1.____________________ On a soccer field, where are the touch lines located?

2.____________________ Which Rookie of the Year was also the most valuable player in the NBA that year?

3.____________________ What is goal tending in basketball?

4.____________________ What is a divot?

5.____________________ What pitcher once struck out ten consecutive batters in a game?

6.____________________ What weights did Kid Gavilan and Tony DeMarco fight as champions?

7.____________________ In boxing, what is a feint?

8.____________________ For what team did Neil Johnston play when he was a three-time scoring champ?

9.____________________ For what accomplishment is the Vardon Trophy awarded?

10.____________________ How many assists did Bobby Orr have in 1970–71, when he set the record?

__________**Score**
(5 points each)

The Ph.D. Level

1.____________________ How much does a hockey puck weigh?

2.____________________ For what team did the "firebrand of hockey" Eddie Shore play?

3.____________________ In 1976–77 the Montreal Canadians lost only eight games. How many did they win?

4.____________________ What football players were nicknamed "Butch Cassidy and the Sundance Kid?"

5.____________________ What football player scored the most points (40) in a single game?

6.____________________ What college holds the record for the longest winning streak (47)?

7.____________________ What is the highest official batting average ever recorded, and who holds the record?

8.____________________ Who was responsible for instituting the tradition of an all-star baseball game?

9.____________________ Name the first relief pitcher to win baseball's MVP award.

10.____________________ How far is a sprint race in horse racing?

__________**Score**
(5 points each)

Test 26

Pulitzer Prizes—Literature

Another important source of recognition for an author is the Pulitzer Prize. This award was endowed by the will of Joseph Pulitzer, founder of the St. Louis Post-Dispatch, *and is administered by Columbia University. Match the authors with their works.*

The B.A. Level

____**1** *All The King's Men*
____**2** *Benjamin Franklin*
____**3** *Abraham Lincoln: The War Years*
____**4** *The Rising Sun*
____**5** *Henry James*
____**6** *The Guns of August*
____**7** *Andersonville*
____**8** *Gödel, Escher, Bach*
____**9** *The Good Earth*
____**10** *Humboldt's Gift*
____**11** *Profiles in Courage*
____**12** *To Kill a Mockingbird*

a John Tolland
b Barbara Tuchman
c Douglas Hofstadter
d Harper Lee
e Saul Bellow
f Robert Penn Warren
g Carl Sandburg
h Pearl S. Buck
i John F. Kennedy
j Carl Van Doren
k Leon Edel
l MacKinlay Kantor

________**Score**
(5 points each)

The M.S. Level

____**1** *The Fixer*
____**2** *Roosevelt and Hopkins*
____**3** *The Magnificent Ambersons*
____**4** *A Death in the Family*
____**5** *The Confessions of Nat Turner*
____**6** *The Armies of the Night*
____**7** *A Bell for Adano*
____**8** *The Yearling*
____**9** *The Age of Jackson*
____**10** *The Bridge of San Luis Rey*
____**11** *The Late George Apley*
____**12** *Arrowsmith*

a Booth Tarkington
b Arthur M. Schlesinger, Jr.
c Bernard Malamud
d Robert E. Sherwood
e Sinclair Lewis
f John Hersey
g Thornton Wilder
h James Agee
i John Phillips Marquand
j Norman Mailer
k Marjorie Kinnan Rawlings
l William Styron

________**Score**
(5 points each)

Test 26

The Ph.D. Level

______ **1** *The Edge of Sadness*	**a** J. P. Lash
______ **2** *Jefferson and His Time*	**b** Allan Nevins
______ **3** *Dragon's Teeth*	**c** C. N. Degler
______ **4** *The Flowering of New England*	**d** Conrad Richter
______ **5** *Eleanor and Franklin*	**e** Wallace Stegner
______ **6** *Guard of Honor*	**f** Dumas Malone
______ **7** *The Killer Angels*	**g** William W. Warner
______ **8** *Neither Black nor White*	**h** Van Wyck Brooks
______ **9** *The Town*	**i** Upton Sinclair
______ **10** *Angle of Repose*	**j** James G. Cozzens
______ **11** *Beautiful Summers*	**k** Edwin O'Connor
______ **12** *Hamilton Fish*	**l** Michael Shaara

____________ **Score**
(5 points each)

Test 27

Tony Awards (Drama and Musicals)—The Women

The Antoinette Perry Award, known as the Tony, honors distinguished achievement in American theater. The award depicts the masks of comedy and tragedy on one side and the profile of actress Antoinette Perry on the other. Match the award winner with her prize-winning show.

The B.A. Level

____ **1** *The King and I*	**a** Carol Channing
____ **2** *The Miracle Worker*	**b** Shirley Booth
____ **3** *A Majority of One*	**c** Judy Holliday
____ **4** *Call Me Madam*	**d** Ellen Burstyn
____ **5** *Hello, Dolly!*	**e** Gertrude Berg
____ **6** *Come Back Little Sheba*	**f** Mary Martin
____ **7** *The Sound of Music*	**g** Anne Bancroft
____ **8** *Same Time, Next Year*	**h** Judith Anderson
____ **9** *Bells are Ringing*	**i** Ethel Merman
____ **10** *Medea*	**j** Gertrude Lawrence

____ **Score**
(5 points each)

The M.S. Level

____ **1** *No Strings*	**a** Julie Harris
____ **2** *Peter Pan*	**b** Rosalind Russell
____ **3** *Separate Tables*	**c** Colleen Dewhurst
____ **4** *The Prime of Miss Jean Brodie*	**d** Angela Lansbury
____ **5** *Ondine*	**e** Margaret Leighton
____ **6** *Damn Yankees*	**f** Diahann Carroll
____ **7** *The Belle of Amherst*	**g** Mary Martin
____ **8** *Mame*	**h** Gwen Verdon
____ **9** *Wonderful Town*	**i** Zoe Caldwell
____ **10** *A Moon for the Misbegotten*	**j** Audrey Hepburn

____ **Score**
(5 points each)

The Ph.D. Level

____ **1** *The Apple Tree*	**a** Julie Harris
____ **2** *The Country Girl*	**b** Katharine Cornell
____ **3** *I Am a Camera*	**c** Elizabeth Seal
____ **4** *Darling of the Day*	**d** Barbara Harris
____ **5** *Antony and Cleopatra*	**e** Glynis Johns
____ **6** *Irma La Douce*	**f** Martita Hunt
____ **7** *A Little Night Music*	**g** Patricia Routledge
____ **8** *The Madwoman of Chaillot*	**h** Beryl Reid
____ **9** *No, No, Nanette*	**i** Uta Hagen
____ **10** *The Killing of Sister George*	**j** Helen Gallagher

____ **Score**
(5 points each)

Test 28

Tony Awards (Drama and Musicals)—The Men

Now we turn our attention to male performers who have won Tony Awards. Match the winner with his prize-winning show.

The B.A. Level

______1 *A Man for All Seasons*
______2 *Camelot*
______3 *Fiddler on the Roof*
______4 *My Fair Lady*
______5 *The Music Man*
______6 *The Seven-Year Itch*
______7 *The Great White Hope*
______8 *Man of La Mancha*
______9 *The Odd Couple*
______10 *Mark Twain Tonight*

a James Earl Jones
b Richard Kiley
c Hal Holbrook
d Rex Harrison
e Richard Burton
f Walter Matthau
g Paul Scofield
h Zero Mostel
i Tom Ewell
j Robert Preston

__________**Score**
(5 points each)

The M.S. Level

______1 *The Teahouse of the August Moon*
______2 *How to Succeed in Business without Really Trying*
______3 *Sunrise at Campobello*
______4 *Purlie*
______5 *Damn Yankees*
______6 *Cyrano de Bergerac*
______7 *I Do! I Do!*
______8 *Pippin*
______9 *Long Day's Journey into Night*
______10 *Anne of the Thousand Days*

a Jose Ferrer
b Ray Walston
c Ben Vereen
d Robert Morse
e Fredric March
f Rex Harrison
g David Wayne
h Ralph Bellamy
i Robert Preston
j Cleavon Little

__________**Score**
(5 points each)

The Ph.D. Level

______1 *Promises, Promises*
______2 *Fanny*
______3 *The Homecoming*
______4 *The School for Wives*
______5 *The Best Man*
______6 *Guys and Dolls*
______7 *The Rothschilds*
______8 *Shenandoah*
______9 *Who's Afraid of Virginia Woolf?*
______10 *Child's Play*

a Walter Slezak
b Hal Linden
c Robert Alda
d Fritz Weaver
e Arthur Hill
f John Cullum
g Brian Bedford
h Paul Rogers
i Jerry Orbach
j Melvyn Douglas

__________**Score**
(5 points each)

Test 29

I Wrote the Words—Lyricists

The story goes that once Mrs. Oscar Hammerstein II was asked if she didn't just love Jerome Kern's "Ol' Man River." She replied that her husband wrote "Ol' Man River," Kern merely wrote "Da-Da-Da Da." This test salutes the men and women who wrote the lyrics of famous songs for Broadway musicals. Match the lyricists with their musicals.

The B.A. Level

____ **1** *Pal Joey*
____ **2** *The Music Man*
____ **3** *Kiss Me Kate*
____ **4** *Hello, Dolly!*
____ **5** *Guys and Dolls*
____ **6** *Funny Girl*
____ **7** *West Side Story*
____ **8** *The Fantasticks*
____ **9** *Promises, Promises*
____ **10** *No Strings*

a Cole Porter
b Frank Loesser
c Tom Jones
d Meredith Wilson
e Richard Rodgers
f Stephen Sondheim
g Hal David
h Lorenz Hart
i Robert Merrill
j Jerry Herman

________ **Score**
(5 points each)

The M.S. Level

____ **1** *Brigadoon*
____ **2** *Fanny*
____ **3** *Li'l Abner*
____ **4** *Stop the World—I Want to Get Off*
____ **5** *Kismet*
____ **6** *Annie Get Your Gun*
____ **7** *Call Me Madam*
____ **8** *Fiddler on the Roof*
____ **9** *Hair*
____ **10** *Pajama Game*

a Johnny Mercer
b Alan Jay Lerner
c Gerome Ragni and James Rado
d Richard Adler and Jerry Ross
e Leslie Bricusse and Anthony Newley
f Sheldon Harnick
g Harold Rome
h Irving Berlin
i Oscar Hammerstein II
j Robert Wright and George Forrest

________ **Score**
(5 points each)

The Ph.D. Level

____ **1** *Man of La Mancha*
____ **2** *Bells are Ringing*
____ **3** *Oliver!*
____ **4** *Gentlemen Prefer Blondes*
____ **5** *Sweet Charity*
____ **6** *High Button Shoes*
____ **7** *Golden Boy*
____ **8** *"1776"*
____ **9** *The Vagabond King*
____ **10** *Good News*

a Betty Comden and Adolph Green
b Leo Robin
c Jule Styne and Sammy Cahn
d B. G. deSylva
e Lee Adams
f Brian Hooker and W. A. Post
g Sherman Edwards
h Dorothy Fields
i Joe Darion
j Lionel Bart

________ **Score**
(5 points each)

Test 30

Once Again—Potpourri

The B.A. Level

1.________________ Where would you find the Mayo Clinic?

2.________________ Where are the crown jewels of England kept?

3.________________ With what country do you associate the currency peseta?

4.________________ What is the title of the wife of an earl?

5.________________ What was the nickname of the Ford Model-T automobile?

6.________________ What was the name of Scarlett O'Hara's Georgia plantation?

7.________________ Who was the first explorer to reach the North Pole?

8.________________ Name the sculptor in Greek legend who fell in love with his statue.

9.________________ Who is *Mad* magazine's "What Me Worry?" hero?

10.________________ What jockey rode Secretariat to the Triple Crown?

________**Score**
(5 points each)

The M.S. Level

1.________________ In James Joyce's *Ulysses,* which character represented the lost Ulysses?

2.________________ Who played Archie the bartender on the radio series *Duffy's Tavern?*

3.________________ Who was the conductor of the Voice of Firestone Orchestra on radio?

4.________________ With what U.S. administration or campaign do you associate the slogan "the Good Neighbor Policy?"

5.________________ Who was three times nominated by the Democrats for the presidency and lost three times?

6.________________ What two nations fought "the opium war" of 1842?

7.________________ Who founded the A & P grocery store chain?

8.________________ Who played and created *Amos 'n Andy?*

9.________________ What is the first name of Mutt of the comic strip Mutt and Jeff?

10.________________ In which story did Sherlock Holmes say "Elementary, my dear Watson"?

________**Score**
(5 points each)

The Ph.D. Level

1.________________ Who is the host of the TV show *Soul Train?*

2.________________ What is caduceus?

3.________________ What is the thing that is sought after in each Hitchcock film?

4.________________ What will be the first day of the twenty-first century?

5.________________ What was the name of William Shakespeare's wife?

6.________________ Who played Huw in *How Green Was My Valley?*

7.________________ What two countries does the Mont Blanc Tunnel join?

8.________________ Who stood in her nightclub and greeted all comers, "Hello, Suckers"?

9.________________ What was the name of the atomic-powered submarine the U.S. Navy sent under the ice at the North Pole?

10.________________ Who signed his paintings with a butterfly?

________**Score**
(5 points each)

Test
31

Solid Gold of the '60's—Vocalists

Rock music changed radically in the sixties. From its primitive beginnings, it became more subtle and sophisticated. Rock now absorbed some of the idioms of serious modern music and even the electrified instruments of avant-garde composers. Just as Elvis Presley dominated rock in the fifties, the propelling force of the rock of the sixties was the Beatles. This test asks you to match vocalists with their million-copies-selling records.

The B.A. Level

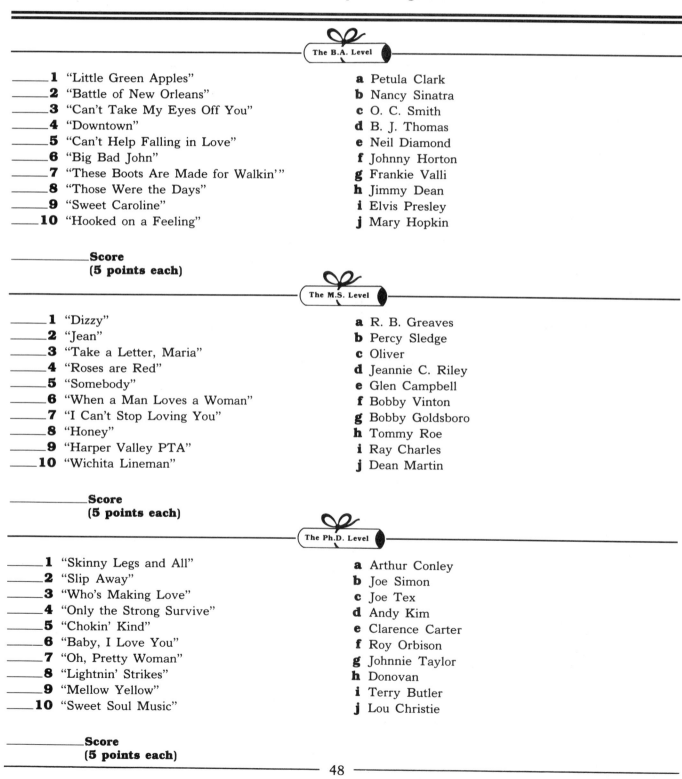

____ **1** "Little Green Apples"
____ **2** "Battle of New Orleans"
____ **3** "Can't Take My Eyes Off You"
____ **4** "Downtown"
____ **5** "Can't Help Falling in Love"
____ **6** "Big Bad John"
____ **7** "These Boots Are Made for Walkin'"
____ **8** "Those Were the Days"
____ **9** "Sweet Caroline"
____ **10** "Hooked on a Feeling"

a Petula Clark
b Nancy Sinatra
c O. C. Smith
d B. J. Thomas
e Neil Diamond
f Johnny Horton
g Frankie Valli
h Jimmy Dean
i Elvis Presley
j Mary Hopkin

______ **Score**
(5 points each)

The M.S. Level

____ **1** "Dizzy"
____ **2** "Jean"
____ **3** "Take a Letter, Maria"
____ **4** "Roses are Red"
____ **5** "Somebody"
____ **6** "When a Man Loves a Woman"
____ **7** "I Can't Stop Loving You"
____ **8** "Honey"
____ **9** "Harper Valley PTA"
____ **10** "Wichita Lineman"

a R. B. Greaves
b Percy Sledge
c Oliver
d Jeannie C. Riley
e Glen Campbell
f Bobby Vinton
g Bobby Goldsboro
h Tommy Roe
i Ray Charles
j Dean Martin

______ **Score**
(5 points each)

The Ph.D. Level

____ **1** "Skinny Legs and All"
____ **2** "Slip Away"
____ **3** "Who's Making Love"
____ **4** "Only the Strong Survive"
____ **5** "Chokin' Kind"
____ **6** "Baby, I Love You"
____ **7** "Oh, Pretty Woman"
____ **8** "Lightnin' Strikes"
____ **9** "Mellow Yellow"
____ **10** "Sweet Soul Music"

a Arthur Conley
b Joe Simon
c Joe Tex
d Andy Kim
e Clarence Carter
f Roy Orbison
g Johnnie Taylor
h Donovan
i Terry Butler
j Lou Christie

______ **Score**
(5 points each)

Test 32

Solid Gold of the '60's—Groups

Rock music is really the province of groups. Sharpen your memory and match the groups with their golden hits.

The B.A. Level

____ **1** "Woman, Woman"	**a** The Cowsills
____ **2** "Stoned Soul Picnic"	**b** Buddy Holly and the Crickets
____ **3** "Hair"	**c** The Beatles
____ **4** "Sugar, Sugar"	**d** Herman's Hermits
____ **5** "That'll Be the Day"	**e** The Union Gap
____ **6** "Spinning Wheel"	**f** The Tokens
____ **7** "The Lion Sleeps"	**g** The 5th Dimension
____ **8** "Can't Buy Me Love"	**h** The Monkees
____ **9** "Mrs. Brown, You've Got a Lovely Daughter"	**i** Blood, Sweat and Tears
____ **10** "Last Train to Clarksville"	**j** The Archies

________ **Score**
(5 points each)

The M.S. Level

____ **1** "Girl Watcher"	**a** The Mamas and the Papas
____ **2** "Yummy, Yummy, Yummy"	**b** The Association
____ **3** "Simon Says"	**c** Ohio Express
____ **4** "In the Year 2525"	**d** The Doors
____ **5** "This Magic Moment"	**e** 1910 Fruitgum Company
____ **6** "California Dreamin'"	**f** Beach Boys
____ **7** "Summer in the City"	**g** Zager and Evans
____ **8** "Good Vibrations"	**h** The Lovin' Spoonful
____ **9** "Light My Fire"	**i** Jay and the Americans
____ **10** "Windy"	**j** The O'Kaysions

________ **Score**
(5 points each)

The Ph.D. Level

____ **1** "Sunshine of Your Love"	**a** Sly and the Family Stone
____ **2** "Born to be Wild"	**b** Edwin Hawkins Singers
____ **3** "Everyday People"	**c** The Young Rascals
____ **4** "Oh Happy Day"	**d** Steppenwolf
____ **5** "Get Together"	**e** The Toys
____ **6** "Satisfaction"	**f** Righteous Brothers
____ **7** "A Lover's Concerto"	**g** Youngbloods
____ **8** "Soul and Inspiration"	**h** The Turtles
____ **9** "Happy Together"	**i** The Rolling Stones
____ **10** "Groovin'"	**j** Cream

________ **Score**
(5 points each)

Test 33

Run and Shoot—Basketball Players of the Year

The game of basketball has changed significantly over the years. Gone are the center jump, the two-hand set shot, and the keyhole. Today's fast game features fast and mobile big men who can shatter a backboard with a slam dunk. The players in this test all have been chosen player-of-the-year in college ball. Match the player with his school.

The B.A. Level

____ **1**	Austin Carr	**a**	Ohio State
____ **2**	Oscar Robinson	**b**	Princeton
____ **3**	Jerry Lucas	**c**	San Francisco
____ **4**	Lewis Alcindor	**d**	Cincinnati
____ **5**	George Mikan	**e**	Kentucky
____ **6**	Bill Russell	**f**	Notre Dame
____ **7**	William Bradley	**g**	Louisiana State
____ **8**	Scott May	**h**	UCLA
____ **9**	Pete Maravitch	**i**	DePaul
____ **10**	Kevin Grevey	**j**	Indiana

________ **Score**
(5 points each)

The M.S. Level

____ **1**	Tom Gola	**a**	UCLA
____ **2**	Bill Walton	**b**	Duke
____ **3**	David Thompson	**c**	Seattle
____ **4**	Arthur Heyman	**d**	Yale
____ **5**	Cazzie Russell	**e**	LaSalle
____ **6**	Ed Macauly	**f**	North Carolina State
____ **7**	Clyde Lovellette	**g**	St. Louis
____ **8**	Anthony Lavelli	**h**	Villanova
____ **9**	Paul Arizin	**i**	Michigan
____ **10**	Elgin Baylor	**j**	Kansas

________ **Score**
(5 points each)

The Ph.D. Level

____ **1**	Robert Houbregs	**a**	Duke
____ **2**	Dick Groat	**b**	Sanford
____ **3**	Walter Hazzard	**c**	Washington
____ **4**	Paul Hogue	**d**	Oklahoma State
____ **5**	Robert Kurland	**e**	UCLA
____ **6**	John Wooden	**f**	North Carolina
____ **7**	Gerald Tucker	**g**	St. Joseph's
____ **8**	Angelo Luisetti	**h**	Oklahoma
____ **9**	George Senesky	**i**	Purdue
____ **10**	Leonard Rosenbluth	**j**	Cincinnati

________ **Score**
(5 points each)

Test 34

Very, Very British

The citizens of Great Britain and the United States both speak English, but they speak it quite differently. Certain words and phrases mean different things in the two countries. Your language test is to match the British word with its American meaning.

The B.A. Level

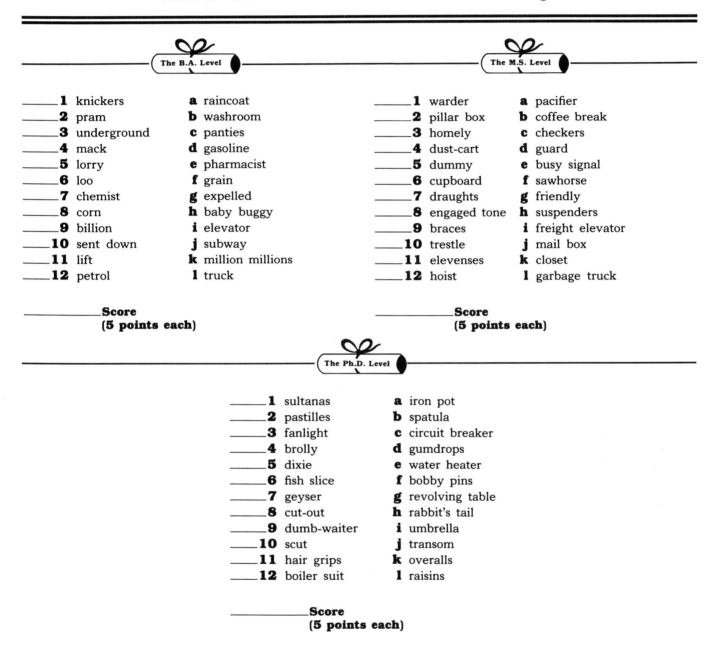

______ **1**	knickers	**a**	raincoat
______ **2**	pram	**b**	washroom
______ **3**	underground	**c**	panties
______ **4**	mack	**d**	gasoline
______ **5**	lorry	**e**	pharmacist
______ **6**	loo	**f**	grain
______ **7**	chemist	**g**	expelled
______ **8**	corn	**h**	baby buggy
______ **9**	billion	**i**	elevator
______ **10**	sent down	**j**	subway
______ **11**	lift	**k**	million millions
______ **12**	petrol	**l**	truck

______ **Score**
(5 points each)

The M.S. Level

______ **1**	warder	**a**	pacifier
______ **2**	pillar box	**b**	coffee break
______ **3**	homely	**c**	checkers
______ **4**	dust-cart	**d**	guard
______ **5**	dummy	**e**	busy signal
______ **6**	cupboard	**f**	sawhorse
______ **7**	draughts	**g**	friendly
______ **8**	engaged tone	**h**	suspenders
______ **9**	braces	**i**	freight elevator
______ **10**	trestle	**j**	mail box
______ **11**	elevenses	**k**	closet
______ **12**	hoist	**l**	garbage truck

______ **Score**
(5 points each)

The Ph.D. Level

______ **1**	sultanas	**a**	iron pot
______ **2**	pastilles	**b**	spatula
______ **3**	fanlight	**c**	circuit breaker
______ **4**	brolly	**d**	gumdrops
______ **5**	dixie	**e**	water heater
______ **6**	fish slice	**f**	bobby pins
______ **7**	geyser	**g**	revolving table
______ **8**	cut-out	**h**	rabbit's tail
______ **9**	dumb-waiter	**i**	umbrella
______ **10**	scut	**j**	transom
______ **11**	hair grips	**k**	overalls
______ **12**	boiler suit	**l**	raisins

______ **Score**
(5 points each)

Test 35

Miscellaneous Movie Trivia

The B.A. Level

1.________________ Who was Katharine Hepburn's character in *The Philadelphia Story?*

2.________________ Who was Janet Gaynor's co-star in *A Star Is Born?*

3.________________ Who was Gene Kelly's piano playing friend in *An American in Paris?*

4.________________ What words did Robert Mitchum have tattooed on his fingers in *The Night of the Hunter?*

5.________________ What role did Bela Lugosi play in *Son of Frankenstein?*

6.________________ Who played *The Dolly Sisters?*

7.________________ Who played the leading role in *Charley's Aunt?*

8.________________ Who played Charlie Chan's (Warner Oland) number one son?

9.________________ Who played Mr. Moto in *Thank You, Mr. Moto?*

10.________________ Who was the government plant spying on Cody Jarrett in *White Heat?*

__________**Score**
(5 points each)

The M.S. Level

1.________________ Henry Fonda was Wyatt Earp and Victor Mature was Doc Holliday in which movie?

2.________________ Who played the Vice-President in *Mr. Smith Goes to Washington?*

3.________________ Pat O'Brien walked the "last mile" with James Cagney in what movie?

4.________________ Who played the sinister housekeeper in *Rebecca?*

5.________________ Who played Jesus Christ in Cecil B. De Mille's 1927 *King of Kings?*

6.________________ Who played Colonel Blimp in *The Life and Death of Colonel Blimp?*

7.________________ What was the name of the character played by Jack Benny in *To Be or Not to Be?*

8.________________ Who were the parents of the communist "viper" in *My Son John?*

9.________________ What was the real name of "The Epic That Never Was"?

10.________________ Which Academy Award winning actor made his film debut as a paraplegic?

__________**Score**
(5 points each)

The Ph.D. Level

1.________________ What famous actor played a not too convincing vampire in *The Return of Doctor X?*

2.________________ Who played De Lawd in *Green Pastures?*

3.________________ Who played George M. Cohan's parents in *Yankee Doodle Dandy?*

4.________________ Which starlet was terrified by the monster in *The Creature from the Black Lagoon?*

5.________________ In which movie did Dorothy Lamour first wear a sarong?

6.________________ When Mr. Deeds went to town, where did he come from?

7.________________ Who played the Creeper in several films, including *House of Horrors?*

8.________________ Who were the *Three Mesquiteers?*

9.________________ Who played the fanatical guru in *Gunga Din?*

10.________________ Who was the narrator of *The Night They Raided Minsky's?*

__________**Score**
(5 points each)

Test 36

For a Few Points

Answer the following questions and take the points.

The B.A. Level

1. For four points name the blood groups.
2. For three points name the Triple Crown of Baseball achievements.
3. For five points name the most common names in the U.S.
4. For two points name the actors who played Brian Piccolo and Gale Sayers in the TV movie *Brian's Song*.
5. For seven points name the Presidents of the U.S. born in Ohio.
6. For four points name the corner squares of the game Monopoly.
7. For five points name the animals eaten by Foxy Loxy.
8. For four points give the first names of the March sisters in *Little Women*.
9. For nine points give the first names of the children of Joseph and Rose Kennedy.
10. For five points name the original *Mission Impossible* force (the actors).

__________**Score**

The M.S. Level

1. For three points name Daniel's brothers who were cast into the furnace.
2. For five points name the comedians who were the "men on the street" interviewed by Steve Allen on the old *Tonight Show*.
3. For six points name the Nobel Prize awards.
4. For eight points name the tokens used in the game of Monopoly.
5. For six points name the graduates of Harvard who became U.S. Presidents.
6. For two points name the rival gangs in the movie *West Side Story*.
7. For four points name the founders of United Artists Corporation.
8. For five points name the movies co-starring Humphrey Bogart and Lauren Bacall.
9. For three points name King Lear's daughters.
10. For two points name Tony Orlando's two female singing companions known as Dawn.

__________**Score**

The Ph.D. Level

1. For six points name the Federal penitentiaries.
2. For three points name the wives of Julius Caesar.
3. For two points name the moons of Mars.
4. For twelve points name the members of the movie *The Dirty Dozen*.
5. For three points name the movies for which Walter Brennan won Academy Awards.
6. For seven points name the liberal arts (classical).
7. For four points name the kinds of human teeth.
8. For three points name the Hindu trinity.
9. For two points what are the names of the Southern Lights and the Northern Lights.
10. For three points name the Little Maids, wards of Ko-Ko in *The Mikado*.

__________**Score**

Test
37

Famous Quotations I—Who Said That?

Words can be used to stir us. Some statements are either so well stated or so meaningful that we never forget them. With that preface, see if you recall who made the following famous statements.

The B.A. Level

_____ **1** "God must love the common man, he made so many of them."
_____ **2** "Religion . . . is the opium of the people."
_____ **3** "Mr. Watson, come here, I want you."
_____ **4** "Mine eyes have seen the glory of the coming of the Lord."
_____ **5** "The world must be made safe for democracy."
_____ **6** "He who can does; he who cannot teaches."
_____ **7** "The business of America is business."
_____ **8** "I shall return."
_____ **9** "You ain't heard nothin' yet, folks."
_____ **10** "You may fire when you are ready, Gridley."

a Julia Ward Howe
b George Dewey
c Karl Marx
d Calvin Coolidge
e Douglas MacArthur
f Alexander Graham Bell
g George Bernard Shaw
h Al Jolson
i Abraham Lincoln
j Woodrow Wilson

__________ **Score**
(5 points each)

The M.S. Level

_____ **1** "I hear America singing, the varied carols I hear."
_____ **2** "Satire is what closes on Saturday night."
_____ **3** "Men seldom make passes at girls who wear glasses."
_____ **4** "Injustice anywhere is a threat to justice everywhere."
_____ **5** "Hope springs eternal in the human breast."
_____ **6** "All animals are equal, but some animals are more equal than others."
_____ **7** "Whether women are better than men, I cannot say—but I can say they are certainly no worse."
_____ **8** "As crude a weapon as the cave man's club, the chemical barrage has been hurled against the fabric of life."
_____ **9** "That action alone is just that does not harm either party to a dispute."
_____ **10** "You don't live in a world all alone. Your brothers are here too."

a Martin Luther King, Jr.
b Albert Schweitzer
c Alexander Pope
d George Orwell
e Rachel Carson
f Golda Meir
g Mohandas Gandhi
h Walt Whitman
i George S. Kaufman
j Dorothy Parker

__________ **Score**
(5 points each)

Test 37

The Ph.D. Level

_____ **1** "All the things I really like to do are either immoral, illegal, or fattening."
_____ **2** "It's what you learn after you know it all that counts."
_____ **3** "Never play cards with a man called Doc. Never eat at a place called Mom's. Never sleep with a woman whose troubles are worse than your own."
_____ **4** "There's always an easy solution to every human problem—neat, plausible, and wrong."
_____ **5** "I cannot forecast to you the action of Russia. It is a riddle wrapped in a mystery inside an enigma."
_____ **6** "We have grasped the mystery of the atom and rejected the Sermon on the Mount."
_____ **7** "Either war is obsolete or men are."
_____ **8** "The justification of majority rule in politics is not to be founded in its ethical superiority."
_____ **9** "When you reread a classic you do not see more in the book than you did before; you see more in you than there was before."
_____ **10** "I shall never believe that God plays dice with the world."

a Albert Einstein
b H. L. Mencken
c Omar Bradley
d Buckminster Fuller
e John Wooden
f Alexander Woollcott
g Winston Churchill
h Walter Lippmann
i Nelson Algren
j Clifton Fadiman

__________ **Score**
(5 points each)

Test 38

The Opera—Ain't It Grand

Most of us owe our knowledge of opera to the Saturday afternoon radio programs from the Met sponsored by Texaco. If we missed the majesty of the staging and costumes, at least we were privileged to hear the music and the voices. This test asks you to match operas with their composers.

The B.A. Level

____ **1** *Carmen*	**a** Gian-Carlo Menotti
____ **2** *The Barber of Seville*	**b** Giacomo Puccini
____ **3** *Tristan und Isolde*	**c** Georges Bizet
____ **4** *The Beggar's Opera*	**d** Richard Wagner
____ **5** *The Marriage of Figaro*	**e** Alexander Borodin
____ **6** *Romeo and Juliet*	**f** Wolfgang Mozart
____ **7** *Prince Igor*	**g** Giacchino Antonio Rossini
____ **8** *Porgy and Bess*	**h** John Gay
____ **9** *Amahl and the Night Visitors*	**i** Charles François Gounod
____ **10** *Tosca*	**j** George Gershwin

________ **Score**
(5 points each)

The M.S. Level

____ **1** *Pelléas et Mélisande*	**a** Nicolai Rimsky-Korsakov
____ **2** *Boris Godunov*	**b** Jacques Offenbach
____ **3** *The Tales of Hoffmann*	**c** Benjamin Britten
____ **4** *Rigoletto*	**d** Richard Strauss
____ **5** *Samson et Dalila*	**e** Serge Prokofiev
____ **6** *Die Fledermaus*	**f** Modest Musorgski
____ **7** *The Love for Three Oranges*	**g** Camille Saint-Saëns
____ **8** *Le Cog d 'Or*	**g** Johann Strauss
____ **9** *Salome*	**i** Claude Debussy
____ **10** *Billy Budd*	**j** Giuseppe Verdi

________ **Score**
(5 points each)

The Ph.D. Level

____ **1** *The Merry Wives of Windsor*	**a** Louis Gruenberg
____ **2** *The Emperor Jones*	**b** Englebert Humperdinck
____ **3** *Fidelio*	**c** Hector Berlioz
____ **4** *The Piper of Hamelin*	**d** Otto Nicolai
____ **5** *Oedipus Rex*	**e** Béla Bartók
____ **6** *Hansel and Gretel*	**f** Ludwig van Beethoven
____ **7** *The Canterbury Pilgrims*	**g** Igor Stravinsky
____ **8** *Benvenuto Cellini*	**h** Victor Herbert
____ **9** *Madeleine*	**i** Victor Messler
____ **10** *Duke Bluebeard's Castle*	**j** Reginald De Koven

________ **Score**
(5 points each)

Test 39

Nicknames of Cities—My Kind of Town

Whether our hometown be large or small, it has some distinction, something about it that makes its citizens proud. Some cities have their nickname assigned by the chamber of commerce, others by songs or poems written to the municipality's praise. You should have no difficulty matching the cities with their popular nicknames.

The B.A. Level

____ **1** Windy City	**a** San Francisco
____ **2** Derby City	**b** Pittsburgh
____ **3** Gotham	**c** Chicago
____ **4** City of the Golden Gate	**d** Reno
____ **5** Kodak City	**e** Atlantic City
____ **6** Biggest Little City in the World	**f** Hartford
____ **7** Convention City	**g** Louisville
____ **8** Insurance City	**h** Milwaukee
____ **9** Smoky City	**i** Rochester
____ **10** Beer Capital of the U.S.	**j** New York

________ **Score**
(5 points each)

The M.S. Level

____ **1** Cigar City	**a** Kansas City, Mo.
____ **2** Mound City	**b** Akron
____ **3** Hub of the Universe	**c** St. Louis
____ **4** Heart of America	**d** Denver
____ **5** Smog City	**e** New Orleans
____ **6** Crescent City	**f** San Antonio
____ **7** Mile-high City	**g** Tampa
____ **8** Rubber Capital of the World	**h** Norfolk
____ **9** Navy Town	**i** Boston
____ **10** Mission City	**j** Los Angeles

________ **Score**
(5 points each)

The Ph.D. Level

____ **1** City Without Clocks	**a** Richmond
____ **2** Glass Capital of the World	**b** Mobile
____ **3** City on Seven Hills	**c** Las Vegas
____ **4** Cereal City	**d** Fort Worth
____ **5** City of Five Flags	**e** Peoria
____ **6** Elm City	**f** Toledo
____ **7** Whiskey Town	**g** Battle Creek
____ **8** Home of Pablum	**h** Grand Rapids
____ **9** Furniture City	**i** New Haven
____ **10** Gate to the West	**j** Evansville

________ **Score**
(5 points each)

Test 40

Miscellaneous Sports Trivia

The B.A. Level

1.__________________ Who beat the Minnesota Vikings in Super Bowl XI?

2.__________________ What football conference does Notre Dame belong to?

3.__________________ What is the penalty for offsides in football?

4.__________________ What college did Calvin Hill attend?

5.__________________ What team did Phil Esposito begin his career with?

6.__________________ How far is the center red line from the blue line in pro hockey?

7.__________________ How many fights did Gene Tunney lose during his boxing career?

8.__________________ Who is the head coach of the University of Kentucky's basketball team? (as of 1984)

9.__________________ Which pitcher won the Cy Young awards for both the N.L. and the A.L.?

10.__________________ Who holds the record for consecutive baseball games played?

__________**Score**
(5 points each)

The M.S. Level

1.__________________ For what events did Mildred "Babe" Didrikson win a gold and silver Olympic medal?

2.__________________ How many times have the winter olympics been held in the U.S.?

3.__________________ What NFL back holds the record for scoring the most points (132) in his rookie season?

4.__________________ With what team did Jim Plunkett begin his pro football career?

5.__________________ What college did Johnny Lujack attend?

6.__________________ What are the chief targets for a knockout punch?

7.__________________ What are the three ways a boxer can win a fight?

8.__________________ What was the first year of the National Invitation Tournament?

9.__________________ Which NBA team set the record for losing the most games (73) in a single season?

10.__________________ What player appeared with more world championship baseball teams than any other?

__________**Score**
(5 points each)

The Ph.D. Level

1.__________________ Only two New York Yankees ever won the Triple Crown. Name them.

2.__________________ Who holds the record for the most triples (36) in a single season?

3.__________________ What baseball player was known as the Flying Dutchman?

4.__________________ How many knockouts did Archie Moore have in his career?

5.__________________ The movie *The Harder They Fall* was a fictionalized version of which heavyweight champion's life story?

6.__________________ When the ABA was dissolved in 1976 which four of its teams joined the NBA?

7.__________________ In what year did Holy Cross win the NCAA basketball championship?

8.__________________ What is the oldest existing golf club in North America?

9.__________________ What do the initials Y.A. stand for in the name Y. A. Tittle?

10.__________________ What was the score of the Jets-Colts Super Bowl III game?

__________**Score**
(5 points each)

Test 41

Allusions—Not Illusions

Frequently in writing and conversation we produce a kind of word economy by using a word or phrase that conveys our meaning. We are using allusions that, supposedly, our audience is completely familiar with. To test this assumption, match the following allusions, or expressions, with the given descriptions.

The B.A. Level

_____ **1** applies to the power of the press
_____ **2** to delete anything that might offend any reader
_____ **3** the one vulnerable spot where one can be reached and hurt
_____ **4** to take goods to a place where it already abounds
_____ **5** refuse to have any dealing with
_____ **6** born to a position of great wealth or station
_____ **7** giving a fancy price for anything, much more than its worth
_____ **8** soothe a troubled spirit
_____ **9** dummy figures set up for the purpose of being knocked down or demolished
_____ **10** beyond the reach of slander or even suspicion

a sent to Coventry
b pay through the nose
c Caesar's wife
d bowdlerize
e Fourth Estate
f oil on the waters
g men of straw
h Achilles heel
i carrying coals to Newcastle
j born to the purple

__________ **Score**
(5 points each)

The M.S. Level

_____ **1** laying plans and promoting one's own interests with others
_____ **2** to praise someone or something to too great an extent
_____ **3** a source of immense wealth
_____ **4** riotously jolly by too much drinking
_____ **5** place of reward for the righteous
_____ **6** one devoted to books and learning and who loves to display it
_____ **7** of tremendous size
_____ **8** to pursue an aim that one can never attain
_____ **9** disorder or confusion
_____ **10** a newly married man

a bonanza
b bacchanalian
c Brobdingnagian
d bluestocking
e at sixes and sevens
f pot of gold
g benedict
h mending fences
i Abraham's bosom
j gilding the lily

__________ **Score**
(5 points each)

Test 41

The Ph.D. Level

______ **1** a literary term for wit
______ **2** a task that is manifestly beyond one's power
______ **3** to put to the test; to find out what one is made of
______ **4** wonderfully absurd
______ **5** suffering disappointments
______ **6** one who is disposed to be partial
______ **7** an enthusiast of Gilbert and Sullivan plays
______ **8** graft
______ **9** insulting
______ **10** pay day is at hand

a beating Banagher
b attic salt
c Savoyard
d bow of Ulysses
e biting the thumb
f baksheesh
g bring to scratch
h all my swans and geese
i look at both sides of the shield
j the ghost walks

____________ **Score**
(5 points each)

Test
42

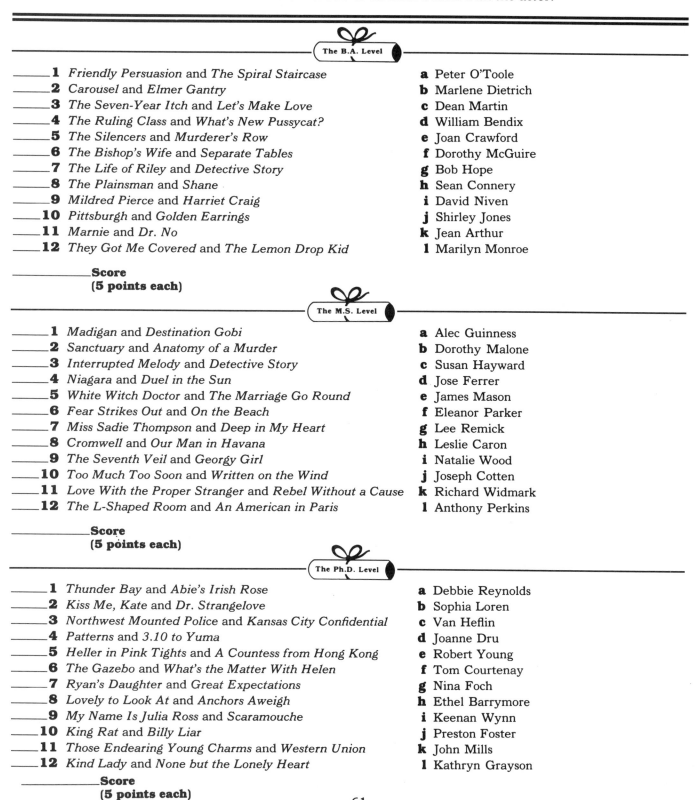

Double Features—Saturday Afternoon's Delight

When you and I were young, before television, Saturday afternoon meant a double feature at the movies with cartoons, newsreels, and perhaps a serial thrown in for good measure. In this test, match a dream double bill of two of an actor's films with the actor.

The B.A. Level

____ **1** *Friendly Persuasion* and *The Spiral Staircase*	**a** Peter O'Toole
____ **2** *Carousel* and *Elmer Gantry*	**b** Marlene Dietrich
____ **3** *The Seven-Year Itch* and *Let's Make Love*	**c** Dean Martin
____ **4** *The Ruling Class* and *What's New Pussycat?*	**d** William Bendix
____ **5** *The Silencers* and *Murderer's Row*	**e** Joan Crawford
____ **6** *The Bishop's Wife* and *Separate Tables*	**f** Dorothy McGuire
____ **7** *The Life of Riley* and *Detective Story*	**g** Bob Hope
____ **8** *The Plainsman* and *Shane*	**h** Sean Connery
____ **9** *Mildred Pierce* and *Harriet Craig*	**i** David Niven
____ **10** *Pittsburgh* and *Golden Earrings*	**j** Shirley Jones
____ **11** *Marnie* and *Dr. No*	**k** Jean Arthur
____ **12** *They Got Me Covered* and *The Lemon Drop Kid*	**l** Marilyn Monroe

________ **Score**
(5 points each)

The M.S. Level

____ **1** *Madigan* and *Destination Gobi*	**a** Alec Guinness
____ **2** *Sanctuary* and *Anatomy of a Murder*	**b** Dorothy Malone
____ **3** *Interrupted Melody* and *Detective Story*	**c** Susan Hayward
____ **4** *Niagara* and *Duel in the Sun*	**d** Jose Ferrer
____ **5** *White Witch Doctor* and *The Marriage Go Round*	**e** James Mason
____ **6** *Fear Strikes Out* and *On the Beach*	**f** Eleanor Parker
____ **7** *Miss Sadie Thompson* and *Deep in My Heart*	**g** Lee Remick
____ **8** *Cromwell* and *Our Man in Havana*	**h** Leslie Caron
____ **9** *The Seventh Veil* and *Georgy Girl*	**i** Natalie Wood
____ **10** *Too Much Too Soon* and *Written on the Wind*	**j** Joseph Cotten
____ **11** *Love With the Proper Stranger* and *Rebel Without a Cause*	**k** Richard Widmark
____ **12** *The L-Shaped Room* and *An American in Paris*	**l** Anthony Perkins

________ **Score**
(5 points each)

The Ph.D. Level

____ **1** *Thunder Bay* and *Abie's Irish Rose*	**a** Debbie Reynolds
____ **2** *Kiss Me, Kate* and *Dr. Strangelove*	**b** Sophia Loren
____ **3** *Northwest Mounted Police* and *Kansas City Confidential*	**c** Van Heflin
____ **4** *Patterns* and *3.10 to Yuma*	**d** Joanne Dru
____ **5** *Heller in Pink Tights* and *A Countess from Hong Kong*	**e** Robert Young
____ **6** *The Gazebo* and *What's the Matter With Helen*	**f** Tom Courtenay
____ **7** *Ryan's Daughter* and *Great Expectations*	**g** Nina Foch
____ **8** *Lovely to Look At* and *Anchors Aweigh*	**h** Ethel Barrymore
____ **9** *My Name Is Julia Ross* and *Scaramouche*	**i** Keenan Wynn
____ **10** *King Rat* and *Billy Liar*	**j** Preston Foster
____ **11** *Those Endearing Young Charms* and *Western Union*	**k** John Mills
____ **12** *Kind Lady* and *None but the Lonely Heart*	**l** Kathryn Grayson

________ **Score**
(5 points each)

Test 43

Noted Political Leaders—Follow Me

Once upon a time people believed that their political leaders could accomplish something. That was probably because they were not so instantly informed of what the leaders were trying to do. Some of the following were able to accomplish something, in certain cases with horrible results. Match the "politicians" with the brief descriptions that identify them.

The B.A. Level

_____**1** notorious for his witch hunt for communists in the government
_____**2** revolutionary, major influence on modern Mexico
_____**3** leader of colonization of Texas
_____**4** West German chancellor after W.W. II
_____**5** first premier of Israel
_____**6** leader of Cuban struggle for independence
_____**7** leader of struggle to win control of Texas from Mexico
_____**8** the Iron Chancellor, united Germany
_____**9** dictator overthrown by Castro
_____**10** his appeasement of Hitler led to Munich Pact

a Stephen F. Austin
b Konrad Adenauer
c Samuel Houston
d José Martí
e Neville Chamberlain
f Joseph McCarthy
g Fulgencio Batista y Zaldívar
h David Ben-Gurion
i Emiliano Zapata
j Otto von Bismarck

__________**Score**
(5 points each)

The M.S. Level

_____**1** prime minister during Suez invasion of 1956
_____**2** founded European Coal and Steel Community
_____**3** first Israeli president
_____**4** "uncrowned King of Ireland"
_____**5** master of mass psychology
_____**6** primarily responsible for the Holocaust
_____**7** enacted national health, nationalized gas, coal, steel
_____**8** founder of modern Zionism
_____**9** founded and headed Gestapo
_____**10** rigorously applied apartheid policy

a Charles Stewart Parnell
b Paul Joseph Goebbels
c Clement Attlee
d Theodor Herzl
e Robert Schuman
f Hendrik F. Verwoerd
g Hermann Goering
h Heinrich Himmler
i Anthony Eden
j Chaim Weizmann

__________**Score**
(5 points each)

The Ph.D. Level

_____**1** championed agrarian interests and westward expansion
_____**2** leading figure in Italian unification movement
_____**3** dictatorial first president of the Indonesian republic
_____**4** the major force of the Congress of Vienna
_____**5** founder of modern Turkey
_____**6** The Great Compromiser
_____**7** regarded as the father of modern China
_____**8** arbiter of post-Napoleonic Europe
_____**9** champion of states' rights
_____**10** first president of the Republic of Korea

a Kemal Atatürk
b Thomas Hart Benton
c Syngman Rhee
d Sun Yat-sen
e Sukarno
f Klemens W.N.L. Metternich
g John C. Calhoun
h Charles de Talleyrand
i Henry Clay
j Giuseppi Garibaldi

__________**Score**
(5 points each)

Test 44

Big Band Vocalists—Now Stepping Up to the Microphone

Once upon a time popular singers were members of some band and their fame was something less than that of the bandleader. For the most part, Frank Sinatra was responsible for the change that brought singers to the forefront. Return now with us to the good old days and match the vocalists with the band.

The B.A. Level

____ **1**	June Christy	**a**	Les Brown
____ **2**	Bing Crosby	**b**	Count Basie
____ **3**	Doris Day	**c**	Kay Kyser
____ **4**	Connie Haines	**d**	Benny Goodman
____ **5**	Peggy Lee	**e**	Jimmy Dorsey
____ **6**	Helen O'Connell	**f**	Charlie Barnet
____ **7**	Billie Holiday	**g**	Stan Kenton
____ **8**	Kay Starr	**h**	Paul Whiteman
____ **9**	Mike Douglas	**i**	Tommy Dorsey
____ **10**	Billy Eckstine	**j**	Artie Shaw

________ **Score**
(5 points each)

The M.S. Level

____ **1**	Mildred Bailey	**a**	Orrin Tucker
____ **2**	Bonnie Baker	**b**	Benny Goodman
____ **3**	Rosemary Clooney	**c**	Tony Pastor
____ **4**	Perry Como	**d**	Glenn Miller
____ **5**	Don Cornell	**e**	Ted Weems
____ **6**	Helen Forrest	**f**	Tommy Dorsey
____ **7**	Merv Griffin	**g**	Red Norvo
____ **8**	Jo Stafford	**h**	Freddy Martin
____ **9**	Martha Tilton	**i**	Sammy Kaye
____ **10**	Marion Hutton	**j**	Artie Shaw

________ **Score**
(5 points each)

The Ph.D. Level

____ **1**	Amy Arnell	**a**	Boyd Raeburn
____ **2**	Dale Evans	**b**	Tommy Tucker
____ **3**	Ella Fitzgerald	**c**	Anson Weeks
____ **4**	Marilyn Maxwell	**d**	Woody Herman
____ **5**	Ginny Powell	**e**	Benny Goodman
____ **6**	Bea Wain	**f**	Chick Webb
____ **7**	Frances Wayne	**g**	Ted Weems
____ **8**	Edythe Wright	**h**	Tommy Dorsey
____ **9**	Helen Ward	**i**	Hal Kemp
____ **10**	Nan Wynn	**j**	Larry Clinton

________ **Score**
(5 points each)

Test 45

The Return of Potpourri

The B.A. Level

1.____________________ What is the slogan of the U.S. Marines?

2.____________________ What is the slogan of Maxwell House coffee?

3.____________________ Who are the enemies of the Federation on the TV series *Star Trek*?

4.____________________ What is the name of the Yale football team's mascot bulldog?

5.____________________ What countries are larger in size than the U.S.?

6.____________________ Where does the following line appear? "Abandon hope all ye who enter here."

7.____________________ In what novel would you find Lady Brett Ashley?

8.____________________ Who founded Tuskegee Institute?

9.____________________ Where is the Tennis Hall of Fame located?

10.____________________ What was the first American movie to tell a story?

__________ **Score**
(5 points each)

The M.S. Level

1.____________________ On what island did Napoleon Bonaparte die?

2.____________________ Who is the cowardly knight who is the head of King ID's army?

3.____________________ Whose portrait appears on a $500 bill?

4.____________________ Who sponsored the radio show *Little Orphan Annie*?

5.____________________ Complete the quote, "Grow old along with me" by giving the line immediately following it.

6.____________________ Christopher Morley has written that a closed door is a _______.

7.____________________ Name the play from which the following quote is taken: "Years from now when you talk about this—and you will—be kind."

8.____________________ What minor comedy of Shakespeare's was turned into an excellent opera by Verdi?

9.____________________ Complete the quote, "In Xanadu did Kubla Khan" by giving the line immediately following it.

10.____________________ Who played Benjamin Franklin in the movie *1776*?

__________ **Score**
(5 points each)

The Ph.D. Level

1.____________________ What is the location of the Hearst castle?

2.____________________ What is a railroad split?

3.____________________ What was Sky King's first name?

4.____________________ An inkhorn word is one which is______.

5.____________________ Where is it? At the head of the stairs to the left of the main entrance stands the *Winged Victory*.

6.____________________ What is the meaning of the following Latin phrase from the Roman Catholic Mass—*Dominus vobiscum*?

7.____________________ Donizetti's opera *Lucia di Lammermoor* is based on a work by_______.

8.____________________ What was the flight of Mohammed from Mecca to Medina called?

9.____________________ What is the highest waterfall in the world?

10.____________________ What was Dickens's last novel?

__________ **Score**
(5 points each)

Test
46

National Capitals—Take Me Home, Country Roads

How is your geography? If you want to win your degrees, you must identify the capitals of these countries.

The B.A. Level

_____	**1** Chile	**a**	Bucharest
_____	**2** Venezuela	**b**	Warsaw
_____	**3** Romania	**c**	Budapest
_____	**4** Yugoslavia	**d**	San Jose
_____	**5** Hungary	**e**	Santiago
_____	**6** Czechoslovakia	**f**	Vienna
_____	**7** Poland	**g**	New Delhi
_____	**8** Belgium	**h**	Belgrade
_____	**9** Austria	**i**	Bogotá
_____	**10** India	**j**	Caracas
_____	**11** Colombia	**k**	Brussels
_____	**12** Costa Rica	**l**	Prague

__________**Score**
(5 points each)

The M.S. Level

_____	**1** New Zealand	**a**	Nicosia
_____	**2** Indonesia	**b**	Ankara
_____	**3** Bulgaria	**c**	Canberra
_____	**4** Cyprus	**d**	Jakarta
_____	**5** Philippines	**e**	Khartoum
_____	**6** Sudan	**f**	Salisbury
_____	**7** Rhodesia	**g**	Addis Ababa
_____	**8** Turkey	**h**	Sofia
_____	**9** Switzerland	**i**	Damascus
_____	**10** Syria	**j**	Wellington
_____	**11** Ethiopia	**k**	Bern
_____	**12** Australia	**l**	Quezon City

__________**Score**
(5 points each)

The Ph.D. Level

_____	**1** Saudi Arabia	**a**	Islamabad
_____	**2** Gabon	**b**	Godthaab
_____	**3** Uganda	**c**	Lusaka
_____	**4** Pakistan	**d**	Colombo
_____	**5** Chad	**e**	Riyadh
_____	**6** Zambia	**f**	Thimphu
_____	**7** Tibet	**g**	Kampala
_____	**8** Senegal	**h**	Rangoon
_____	**9** Sri Lanka	**i**	Dakar
_____	**10** Greenland	**j**	Libreville
_____	**11** Burma	**k**	Lhasa
_____	**12** Bhutan	**l**	Fort-Lamy

__________**Score**
(5 points each)

Test 47

Who Are You Really?

Many entertainers have found it useful to change their names. It was often believed that their real names did not project the appropriate image. Match the well-known celebrities with their not so well known original identities.

The B.A. Level

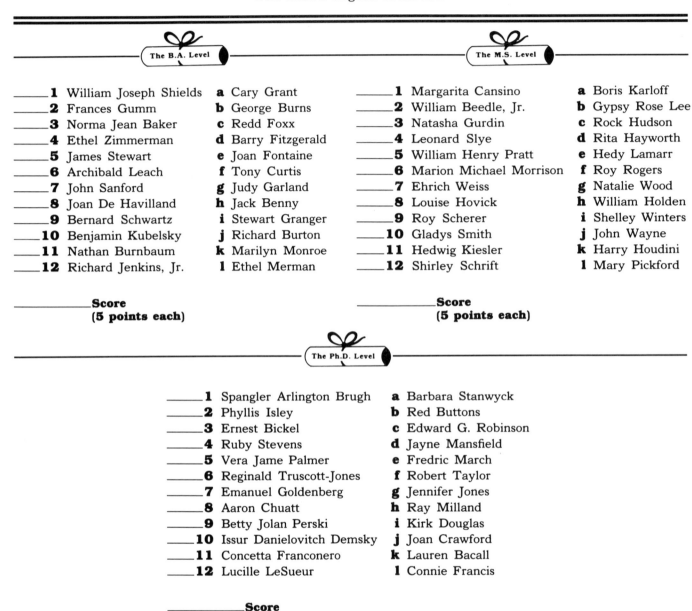

____	**1** William Joseph Shields	**a**	Cary Grant
____	**2** Frances Gumm	**b**	George Burns
____	**3** Norma Jean Baker	**c**	Redd Foxx
____	**4** Ethel Zimmerman	**d**	Barry Fitzgerald
____	**5** James Stewart	**e**	Joan Fontaine
____	**6** Archibald Leach	**f**	Tony Curtis
____	**7** John Sanford	**g**	Judy Garland
____	**8** Joan De Havilland	**h**	Jack Benny
____	**9** Bernard Schwartz	**i**	Stewart Granger
____	**10** Benjamin Kubelsky	**j**	Richard Burton
____	**11** Nathan Burnbaum	**k**	Marilyn Monroe
____	**12** Richard Jenkins, Jr.	**l**	Ethel Merman

__________**Score**
(5 points each)

The M.S. Level

____	**1** Margarita Cansino	**a**	Boris Karloff
____	**2** William Beedle, Jr.	**b**	Gypsy Rose Lee
____	**3** Natasha Gurdin	**c**	Rock Hudson
____	**4** Leonard Slye	**d**	Rita Hayworth
____	**5** William Henry Pratt	**e**	Hedy Lamarr
____	**6** Marion Michael Morrison	**f**	Roy Rogers
____	**7** Ehrich Weiss	**g**	Natalie Wood
____	**8** Louise Hovick	**h**	William Holden
____	**9** Roy Scherer	**i**	Shelley Winters
____	**10** Gladys Smith	**j**	John Wayne
____	**11** Hedwig Kiesler	**k**	Harry Houdini
____	**12** Shirley Schrift	**l**	Mary Pickford

__________**Score**
(5 points each)

The Ph.D. Level

____	**1** Spangler Arlington Brugh	**a**	Barbara Stanwyck
____	**2** Phyllis Isley	**b**	Red Buttons
____	**3** Ernest Bickel	**c**	Edward G. Robinson
____	**4** Ruby Stevens	**d**	Jayne Mansfield
____	**5** Vera Jame Palmer	**e**	Fredric March
____	**6** Reginald Truscott-Jones	**f**	Robert Taylor
____	**7** Emanuel Goldenberg	**g**	Jennifer Jones
____	**8** Aaron Chuatt	**h**	Ray Milland
____	**9** Betty Jolan Perski	**i**	Kirk Douglas
____	**10** Issur Danielovitch Demsky	**j**	Joan Crawford
____	**11** Concetta Franconero	**k**	Lauren Bacall
____	**12** Lucille LeSueur	**l**	Connie Francis

__________**Score**
(5 points each)

Test 48

If They Asked Me I Could Write a . . . Poem

Roses are Red
Violets are Blue
Who wrote the poems
Oh, tell me true

The B.A. Level

____ **1** "The Rape of the Lock"	**a** Walt Whitman
____ **2** "Elegy Written in a Country Churchyard"	**b** Emily Dickinson
____ **3** "A Red, Red Rose"	**c** Alexander Pope
____ **4** "The Rime of the Ancient Mariner"	**d** Thomas Gray
____ **5** "Ode to a Nightingale"	**e** Robert Browning
____ **6** "Out of the Cradle Endlessly Rocking"	**f** Samuel Taylor Coleridge
____ **7** "Morte d'Arthur"	**g** Robert Burns
____ **8** "My Last Duchess"	**h** Robert Frost
____ **9** "I Died for Beauty"	**i** John Keats
____ **10** "Mending Wall"	**j** Alfred Lord Tennyson

________ **Score**
(5 points each)

The M.S. Level

____ **1** "Proud Maisie"	**a** George Gordon, Lord Byron
____ **2** "So, We'll Go No More A-roving"	**b** A. E. Housman
____ **3** "Ode to the West Wind"	**c** Walter de la Mare
____ **4** "To An Athlete Dying Young"	**d** Ezra Pound
____ **5** "Leda and the Swan"	**e** T. S. Eliot
____ **6** "The Listeners"	**f** Archibald MacLeish
____ **7** "The Idea of Order at Key West"	**g** Percy Bysshe Shelley
____ **8** "A Virginal"	**h** Sir Walter Scott
____ **9** "Journey of the Magi"	**i** William Butler Yeats
____ **10** "The End of the World"	**j** Wallace Stevens

________ **Score**
(5 points each)

The Ph.D. Level

____ **1** "The Deserted Village"	**a** Robert Lowell
____ **2** "I Traveled Among Unknown Men"	**b** Oliver Goldsmith
____ **3** "Each and All"	**c** Dylan Thomas
____ **4** "To Helen, Helen, Thy Beauty Is to Me"	**d** Gerard Manley Hopkins
____ **5** "Heaven—Haven"	**e** William Wordsworth
____ **6** "The Curate's Kindness"	**f** Ralph Waldo Emerson
____ **7** "Apology for Bad Dreams"	**g** Robert Graves
____ **8** "To Juan at the Winter Solstice"	**h** Edgar Allan Poe
____ **9** "In My Craft or Sullen Art"	**i** Thomas Hardy
____ **10** "Mr. Edwards and the Spider"	**j** Robinson Jeffers

________ **Score**
(5 points each)

Test 49

Rah, Rah Team—College Nicknames

Cheer, cheer for your college team, whether it be Eagles, Broncos, Bulldogs, Crusaders, Boiler-makers, or whatever. Sports fans and trivia buffs should have no difficulty in matching colleges with their nicknames.

The B.A. Level

____ **1** Panthers	**a** Cornell
____ **2** Orange Men	**b** Minnesota
____ **3** Big Red	**c** Columbia
____ **4** Bruins	**d** Michigan
____ **5** Gophers	**e** Kansas
____ **6** Nittany Lions	**f** Syracuse
____ **7** Wolverines	**g** North Carolina
____ **8** Spartans	**h** UCLA
____ **9** Jayhawks	**i** Penn State
____ **10** Tar Heels	**j** Pittsburgh
____ **11** Sooners	**k** Oklahoma
____ **12** Lions	**l** Michigan State

____________ **Score**
(5 points each)

The M.S. Level

____ **1** Rebels	**a** Arizona
____ **2** Volunteers	**b** Brigham Young
____ **3** Cornhuskers	**c** Tennessee
____ **4** Wildcats	**d** Mississippi
____ **5** Badgers	**e** Oregon State
____ **6** Cavaliers	**f** Nebraska
____ **7** Buffaloes	**g** Clemson
____ **8** Cougars	**h** Washington
____ **9** Beavers	**i** Colorado
____ **10** Huskies	**j** Oregon
____ **11** Tigers	**k** Wisconsin
____ **12** Ducks	**l** Virginia

____________ **Score**
(5 points each)

The Ph.D. Level

____ **1** Salukis	**a** New Mexico
____ **2** Cadets	**b** Rutgers
____ **3** Fightin' Blue Hens	**c** Idaho
____ **4** Rockets	**d** Slippery Rock
____ **5** Scarlet Knights	**e** Indiana State
____ **6** Engineers	**f** Wichita State
____ **7** Palidans	**g** Citadel
____ **8** Lobos	**h** Muhlenberg
____ **9** Shockers	**i** Southern Illinois
____ **10** Sycamores	**j** Furman
____ **11** Mules	**k** Lehigh
____ **12** Vandals	**l** Delaware

____________ **Score**
(5 points each)

Test 50

Miscellaneous Movie Trivia

The B.A. Level

1.____________ Who played Cecil Rhodes in *Rhodes of Africa?*

2.____________ Who played the title role in the 1934 version of *David Copperfield?*

3.____________ Who played the faithful black servant in *The Man Who Shot Liberty Valance?*

4.____________ What was the name of the movie about John F. Kennedy's wartime experience?

5.____________ Who was the cowardly lion opposite Judy Garland in *The Wizard of Oz?*

6.____________ What city was featured in *Three Coins in the Fountain?*

7.____________ Who played the title role in *Sergeant York?*

8.____________ Who played the mayor's wife in *The Music Man?*

9.____________ Who played the English butler in *Ruggles of Red Gap?*

10.____________ Who played the principal of St. Mary's in *The Bells of St. Mary?*

________**Score**
(5 points each)

The M.S. Level

1.____________ Who was the bloated Wall Street shark in *You Can't Take It with You?*

2.____________ Who was the narrator of the *Solid Gold Cadillac?*

3.____________ Who played the supposed cat-woman in *Cat People?*

4.____________ Who played Sherlock Holmes's dangerous female adversary in *Spider Woman?*

5.____________ Who played Captain Robert Falcon Scott in *Scott of the Antarctic?*

6.____________ Who played Fredric March and Myrna Loy's daughter in *The Best Years of Our Lives?*

7.____________ Who was the child star of *The Little Colonel?*

8.____________ What is the heroine of *Genevieve?*

9.____________ Who played Joan Crawford's adversary in *Johnny Guitar?*

10.____________ In which movie did Fred Astaire dance on the walls and ceilings?

________**Score**
(5 points each)

The Ph.D. Level

1.____________ Who played Jack the Ripper in *The Lodger?*

2.____________ In a Western movie sense, what do Walter Brennan and Paul Newman have in common?

3.____________ Who narrated *The Legend of Sleepy Hollow?*

4.____________ In what foreign movie did a knight play chess with Death?

5.____________ Who was the sly landlord Mr. Appopolous in *My Sister Eileen?*

6.____________ Name the movie that featured John Houseman as Professor Kingsfield?

7.____________ In what movie did Myrna Loy play Shirley Temple's sister?

8.____________ In which Hitchcock movie did Claude Rains say, "Mother, I am married to an American agent"?

9.____________ Who composed the score for the movie *Ivanhoe?*

10.____________ In *The Greatest Show on Earth,* who played the part of the famous clown Emmett Kelly?

________**Score**
(5 points each)

Test 51

For a Few Points—Again

Answer the questions and take the points.

The B.A. Level

1. For three points name the kingdoms of nature.
2. For five points name the nations of Scandinavia.
3. For two points give the first names of the singing team the Carpenters.
4. For eleven points name the Confederate states.
5. For three points name the Earp brothers.
6. For four points name the Banana Splits (a children's TV show).
7. For five points name the colors of Life Savers candy.
8. For four points name Pythagoras's basic elements.
9. For four points give the first names of the Lennon Sisters.
10. For six points name the Beach Boys.

__________**Score**

The M.S. Level

1. For seven points name the states of Australia.
2. For three points name the novels of the *Bounty* trilogy.
3. For thirteen points name the original colonies.
4. For two points give the first names of the Dodge brothers.
5. For six points name the weapons used in the game of Clue.
6. For five points name the baseball commissioners prior to 1984.
7. For two points name the dual role of Lee Marvin in the movie *Cat Ballou.*
8. For three points name the top orange-producing states in the U.S.
9. For two points give the first names of the Everly Brothers.
10. For five points name the permanent members of the U.N. Security Council.

__________**Score**

The Ph.D. Level

1. For three points name the astronauts who were killed when a fire occurred inside Apollo 1 space capsule.
2. For five points name the Indian tribes who called themselves "civilized."
3. For three points name Noah's sons.
4. For seven points name the works of mercy.
5. For four points name the Ames brothers.
6. For two points name Cinderella's two stepsisters in the Disney cartoon feature movie.
7. For six points name the Balkan states.
8. For five points name the five books of Moses.
9. For three points name the three actors who have played James Bond's arch-enemy Ernst Stavro Blofeld.
10. For twelve points name the animal designations of the Chinese calendar.

__________**Score**

Test
52

And the Winner Is—Best Supportin

Match the Academy Award-winning supporting actress with the movie for whic

The B.A. Level

____1	*Julia*	**a**	Goldie Hawn
____2	*Murder on the Orient Express*	**b**	Patty Duke
____3	*West Side Story*	**c**	Eva Marie Saint
____4	*On the Waterfront*	**d**	Rita Moreno
____5	*Shampoo*	**e**	Miyoshi Umeki
____6	*The Miracle Worker*	**f**	Donna Reed
____7	*From Here to Eternity*	**g**	Vanessa Redgrave
____8	*Cactus Flower*	**h**	Lee Grant
____9	*Sayonara*	**i**	Estelle Parsons
____10	*Bonnie and Clyde*	**j**	Ingrid Bergman

________**Score**
(5 points each)

The M.S. Level

____1	*The Grapes of Wrath*	**a**	Helen Hayes
____2	*East of Eden*	**b**	Shelley Winters
____3	*The VIPs*	**c**	Sandy Dennis
____4	*All The King's Men*	**d**	Jo Van Fleet
____5	*Airport*	**e**	Mercedes McCambridge
____6	*The Last Picture Show*	**f**	Gloria Grahame
____7	*Who's Afraid of Virginia Woolf?*	**g**	Cloris Leachman
____8	*A Patch of Blue*	**h**	Kim Hunter
____9	*The Bad and the Beautiful*	**i**	Margaret Rutherford
____10	*A Streetcar Named Desire*	**j**	Jane Darwell

________**Score**
(5 points each)

The Ph.D. Level

____1	*In Old Chicago*	**a**	Ethel Barrymore
____2	*Key Largo*	**b**	Josephine Hull
____3	*Jezebel*	**c**	Anne Baxter
____4	*None But the Lonely Heart*	**d**	Alice Brady
____5	*Harvey*	**e**	Wendy Hiller
____6	*The Razor's Edge*	**f**	Celeste Holm
____7	*Butterflies Are Free*	**g**	Beatrice Straight
____8	*Network*	**h**	Fay Bainter
____9	*Gentleman's Agreement*	**i**	Eileen Heckart
____10	*Separate Tables*	**j**	Claire Trevor

________**Score**
(5 points each)

Test 53

And the Winner Is—Best Supporting Actor

Match the Academy Award-winning supporting actor with the movie for which he won the award.

The B.A. Level

______ **1** *Cabaret*	**a** Robert De Niro
______ **2** *The Paper Chase*	**b** George Kennedy
______ **3** *The Sunshine Boys*	**c** George Chakiris
______ **4** *Hud*	**d** Red Buttons
______ **5** *Sayonara*	**e** George Burns
______ **6** *All The President's Men*	**f** John Houseman
______ **7** *West Side Story*	**g** Melvyn Douglas
______ **8** *They Shoot Horses, Don't They?*	**h** Jason Robards
______ **9** *Cool Hand Luke*	**i** Joel Grey
______ **10** *The Godfather, Part II*	**j** Gig Young

__________ **Score**
(5 points each)

The M.S. Level

______ **1** *Viva Zapata!*	**a** Frank Sinatra
______ **2** *Going My Way*	**b** Donald Crisp
______ **3** *A Streetcar Named Desire*	**c** Edmund Gwenn
______ **4** *How Green Was My Valley*	**d** George Sanders
______ **5** *The Fortune Cookie*	**e** Walter Matthau
______ **6** *From Here to Eternity*	**f** Walter Huston
______ **7** *Miracle on 34th Street*	**g** Barry Fitzgerald
______ **8** *All About Eve*	**h** Jack Lemmon
______ **9** *The Treasure of the Sierra Madre*	**i** Karl Malden
______ **10** *Mister Roberts*	**j** Anthony Quinn

__________ **Score**
(5 points each)

The Ph.D. Level

______ **1** *The Big Country*	**a** Edmond O'Brien
______ **2** *Johnny Eager*	**b** Burl Ives
______ **3** *The Best Years of Our Lives*	**c** Thomas Mitchell
______ **4** *The Barefoot Contessa*	**d** James Dunn
______ **5** *Sweet Bird of Youth*	**e** Anthony Quinn
______ **6** *The More The Merrier*	**f** Charles Coburn
______ **7** *Lust for Life*	**g** Walter Brennan
______ **8** *A Tree Grows in Brooklyn*	**h** Ed Begley
______ **9** *Kentucky*	**i** Van Heflin
______ **10** *Stagecoach*	**j** Harold Russell

__________ **Score**
(5 points each)

Test
54

What's in a Name—Musicals

While it is fairly easy to remember the performers in musicals, the characters they played escape us. However, the characters chosen for this test are quite memorable, so you should have little trouble identifying the musical in which they were featured.

The B.A. Level

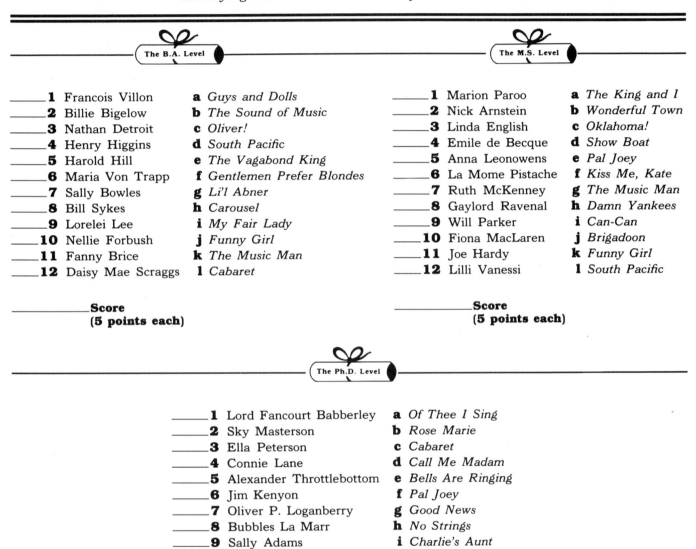

______	**1** Francois Villon	**a**	*Guys and Dolls*
______	**2** Billie Bigelow	**b**	*The Sound of Music*
______	**3** Nathan Detroit	**c**	*Oliver!*
______	**4** Henry Higgins	**d**	*South Pacific*
______	**5** Harold Hill	**e**	*The Vagabond King*
______	**6** Maria Von Trapp	**f**	*Gentlemen Prefer Blondes*
______	**7** Sally Bowles	**g**	*Li'l Abner*
______	**8** Bill Sykes	**h**	*Carousel*
______	**9** Lorelei Lee	**i**	*My Fair Lady*
______	**10** Nellie Forbush	**j**	*Funny Girl*
______	**11** Fanny Brice	**k**	*The Music Man*
______	**12** Daisy Mae Scraggs	**l**	*Cabaret*

__________**Score**
(5 points each)

The M.S. Level

______	**1** Marion Paroo	**a**	*The King and I*
______	**2** Nick Arnstein	**b**	*Wonderful Town*
______	**3** Linda English	**c**	*Oklahoma!*
______	**4** Emile de Becque	**d**	*Show Boat*
______	**5** Anna Leonowens	**e**	*Pal Joey*
______	**6** La Mome Pistache	**f**	*Kiss Me, Kate*
______	**7** Ruth McKenney	**g**	*The Music Man*
______	**8** Gaylord Ravenal	**h**	*Damn Yankees*
______	**9** Will Parker	**i**	*Can-Can*
______	**10** Fiona MacLaren	**j**	*Brigadoon*
______	**11** Joe Hardy	**k**	*Funny Girl*
______	**12** Lilli Vanessi	**l**	*South Pacific*

__________**Score**
(5 points each)

The Ph.D. Level

______	**1** Lord Fancourt Babberley	**a**	*Of Thee I Sing*
______	**2** Sky Masterson	**b**	*Rose Marie*
______	**3** Ella Peterson	**c**	*Cabaret*
______	**4** Connie Lane	**d**	*Call Me Madam*
______	**5** Alexander Throttlebottom	**e**	*Bells Are Ringing*
______	**6** Jim Kenyon	**f**	*Pal Joey*
______	**7** Oliver P. Loganberry	**g**	*Good News*
______	**8** Bubbles La Marr	**h**	*No Strings*
______	**9** Sally Adams	**i**	*Charlie's Aunt*
______	**10** Vera Simpson	**j**	*Follow the Girls*
______	**11** Clifford Bradshaw	**k**	*Guys and Dolls*
______	**12** Barbara Woodruff	**l**	*Louisiana Purchase*

__________**Score**
(5 points each)

Test 55

You Throw da Ball, I'll Ketch It—Baseball Batteries

Over the years there have been many successful pitcher-catcher teams in baseball. The ones chosen for this test are not necessarily the most prominent but they were successful combinations. Match the pitcher with his catcher.

The B.A. Level

____ **1** Steve Carlton	**a** Johnny Roseboro
____ **2** Don Newcombe	**b** Jerry Grote
____ **3** Whitey Ford	**c** Tom Haller
____ **4** Don Drysdale	**d** Tim McCarver
____ **5** Juan Marichal	**e** Randy Hundley
____ **6** Ferguson Jenkins	**f** Thurman Munson
____ **7** Bob Gibson	**g** Elston Howard
____ **8** Tom Seaver	**h** Jake Gibbs
____ **9** Mel Stottlemyre	**i** Roy Campanella
____ **10** Ron Guidry	**j** Ted Simmons

____ **Score**
(5 points each)

The M.S. Level

____ **1** Warren Spahn	**a** Sherm Lollar
____ **2** Billy Pierce	**b** Andy Seminick
____ **3** Robin Roberts	**c** Ernie Lombardi
____ **4** Sal Maglie	**d** Bill Dickey
____ **5** Bob Lemon	**e** Mickey Cochrane
____ **6** Vic Raschi	**f** Del Crandall
____ **7** Mickey Lolich	**g** Wes Westrum
____ **8** Lefty Grove	**h** Bill Freehan
____ **9** Lefty Gomez	**i** Jim Hegan
____ **10** Bucky Walters	**j** Yogi Berra

____ **Score**
(5 points each)

The Ph.D. Level

____ **1** Lon Warneke	**a** Ray Schalk
____ **2** Van Lingle Mungo	**b** Steve O'Neill
____ **3** Eddie Cicotte	**c** Birdie Tebbetts
____ **4** Stan Covelski	**d** Gabby Hartnett
____ **5** Bob Shawkey	**e** Johnny Kling
____ **6** Wes Ferrell	**f** Al Lopez
____ **7** Hal Newhouser	**g** Zack Taylor
____ **8** Dazzy Vance	**h** Muddy Ruel
____ **9** Three-Finger Brown	**i** Roger Bresnahan
____ **10** Christy Mathewson	**j** Luke Sewell

____ **Score**
(5 points each)

Test
56

Almost Synonyms

From each of the following group of four words select the word whose meaning is most nearly the same as the given word.

The B.A. Level

_____ **1** salient: **a.** unimportant **b.** prominent **c.** reviled **d.** discernible
_____ **2** condone: **a.**blame **b.** forgive **c.** console **d.** disapprove
_____ **3** prototype: **a.** similitude **b.** model **c.** printing process **d.** vanguard of a movement
_____ **4** viscous: **a.** acid **b.** poisonous **c.** sticky **d.** sharp
_____ **5** disparage: **a.** divide **b.** dismiss **c.** belittle **d.** discourage
_____ **6** innocuous: **a.** trusting **b.** childish **c.** truthful **d.** harmless
_____ **7** gauche: **a.** a Hungarian meat dish **b.** a method of painting **c.** awkward **d.** an Argentine cowboy
_____ **8** perquisite: **a.** requirement **b.** gratuity **c.** direction **d.** perfection
_____ **9** impinge: **a.** strike **b.** paint **c.** make thin **d.** foster
_____ **10** fiat: **a.** failure **b.** certainty **c.** decree **d.** festival

_____ **Score**
(5 points each)

The M.S. Level

_____ **1** amorphous: **a.** breakable **b.** shapeless **c.** light **d.** microscope
_____ **2** subsidence: **a.** government grant **b.** means of support **c.** inadequate provision **d.** abatement
_____ **3** inexorable: **a.** just **b.** lax **c.** relentless **d.** unwritten
_____ **4** dilettante: **a.** despot **b.** amateur **c.** culture **d.** conqueror
_____ **5** ellipsis: **a.** a plane curve **b.** the omission of one or more words **c.** a disease **d.** a huge animal
_____ **6** stolid: **a.** dull **b.** sullen **c.** active **d.** adroit
_____ **7** moribund: **a.** dying **b.** curious **c.** stubborn **d.** reclining
_____ **8** bane: **a.** shame **b.** poison **c.** joy **d.** perfume
_____ **9** fortuitous: **a.** resolute **b.** fortunate **c.** courageous **d.** chance
_____ **10** transcend: **a.** cut through **b.** rise above **c.** pass across **d.** transfer

_____ **Score**
(5 points each)

The Ph.D. Level

_____ **1** didactic: **a.** figurative **b.** moralistic **c.** overpowering **d.** demoralizing
_____ **2** foulard: **a.** calumny **b.** textile **c.** young rooster **d.** knave
_____ **3** napery: **a.** table linen **b.** trickery **c.** part of the neck **d.** downy surface
_____ **4** mendacious: **a.** beggarly **b.** false **c.** threatening **d.** offensive
_____ **5** germane: **a.** incipient **b.** teutonic **c.** inconsequential **d.** relevant
_____ **6** ostensibly: **a.** forcibly **b.** with constraint **c.** professedly **d.** pretentiously
_____ **7** acumen: **a.** greed **b.** sagacity **c.** adverse criticism **d.** precision
_____ **8** inveigh: **a.** denounce **b.** praise **c.** agree **d.** estimate
_____ **9** overt: **a.** illegal **b.** hidden **c.** circular **d.** unconcealed
_____ **10** lacuna: **a.** a gap **b.** a gem **c.** a body of water **d.** a statue

_____ **Score**
(5 points each)

Test 57

Perry Mason Cases—The Lucky Lawyer

This test requires a real Erle Stanley Gardner fanatic. You are asked to finish the title of each of the following Perry Mason cases.

The B.A. Level

____ **1** *The Lucky . . .*	**a** *Cat*
____ **2** *The Haunted . . .*	**b** *Gorilla*
____ **3** *The Lazy . . .*	**c** *Partner*
____ **4** *The Caretaker's . . .*	**d** *Wife*
____ **5** *The Grinning . . .*	**e** *Daughter*
____ **6** *The Silent . . .*	**f** *Bridegroom*
____ **7** *The Dubious . . .*	**g** *Legs*
____ **8** *The Curious . . .*	**h** *Lover*
____ **9** *The Duplicate . . .*	**i** *Bride*
____ **10** *The Half-Wakened . . .*	**j** *Husband*

____ **Score**
(5 points each)

The M.S. Level

____ **1** *The Long-Legged . . .*	**a** *Doll*
____ **2** *The Singing . . .*	**b** *Nurse*
____ **3** *The Empty . . .*	**c** *Redhead*
____ **4** *The Black-Eyed . . .*	**d** *Skirt*
____ **5** *The Fan-Dancer's . . .*	**e** *Candle*
____ **6** *The Counterfeit . . .*	**f** *Claws*
____ **7** *The Velvet . . .*	**g** *Eye*
____ **8** *The Footloose . . .*	**h** *Blonde*
____ **9** *The Restless . . .*	**i** *Models*
____ **10** *The Fugitive . . .*	**j** *Horse*

____ **Score**
(5 points each)

The Ph.D. Level

____ **1** *The Lame . . .*	**a** *Tin*
____ **2** *The Rolling . . .*	**b** *Niece*
____ **3** *The Empty . . .*	**c** *Canary*
____ **4** *The Drowning . . .*	**d** *Fortune*
____ **5** *The Careless . . .*	**e** *Corpse*
____ **6** *The Sleepwalker's . . .*	**f** *Bones*
____ **7** *The Golddigger's . . .*	**g** *Witness*
____ **8** *The Runaway . . .*	**h** *Duck*
____ **9** *The One-Eyed . . .*	**i** *Purse*
____ **10** *The Phantom . . .*	**j** *Kitten*

____ **Score**
(5 points each)

Test
58

And Then I Directed

How well do you know the work of directors? In this test select the movie that was not *the work of the given director.*

The B.A. Level

______1 George Cukor: **a.** *Adam's Rib* **b.** *Johnny Belinda* **c.** *My Fair Lady* **d.** *The Philadelphia Story*
______2 Otto Preminger: **a.** *Advise and Consent* **b.** *The Moon Is Blue* **c.** *Stalag 17* **d.** *The Detective*
______3 John Ford: **a.** *The Razor's Edge* **b.** *The Quiet Man* **c.** *The Last Hurrah* **d.** *How Green Was My Valley*
______4 Alfred Hitchcock: **a.** *North by Northwest* **b.** *This Gun for Hire* **c.** *Rear Window* **d.** *Strangers on a Train*
______5 John Huston: **a.** *High Sierra* **b.** *The Treasure of the Sierra Madre* **c.** *The Maltese Falcon* **d.** *The African Queen*
______6 Orson Welles: **a.** *Sullivan's Travels* **b.** *The Magnificent Ambersons* **c.** *Macbeth* **d.** *Citizen Kane*
______7 Billy Wilder: **a.** *The Apartment* **b.** *Witness for the Prosecution* **c.** *The Hucksters* **d.** *Irma La Douce*
______8 Frank Capra: **a.** *It Happened One Night* **b.** *It's a Wonderful Life* **c.** *Mr. Blanding Builds His Dream House* **d.** *Lost Horizon*
______9 Cecil B. DeMille: **a.** *The Sign of the Cross* **b.** *Intolerance* **c.** *Union Pacific* **d.** *Reap the Wild Wind*
______10 Mike Nichols: **a.** *Who's Afraid of Virginia Woolf?* **b.** *Catch 22* **c.** *Carnal Knowledge* **d.** *April Fools*

______**Score**
(5 points each)

The M.S. Level

______1 Roger Vadim: **a.** *Barbarella* **b.** *Pretty Maids All in a Row* **c.** *Viva Maria* **d.** *And God Created Woman*
______2 Robert Wise: **a.** *West Side Story* **b.** *Camelot* **c.** *The Sound of Music* **d.** *The Sand Pebbles*
______3 Elia Kazan: **a.** *A Face in the Crowd* **b.** *Gentleman's Agreement* **c.** *The Last Angry Man* **d.** *East of Eden*
______4 Vincente Minnelli: **a.** *The Wizard of Oz* **b.** *An American in Paris* **c.** *Gigi* **d.** *The Bandwagon*
______5 Roberto Rossellini: **a.** *Open City* **b.** *The Red Desert* **c.** *Paisan* **d.** *Stromboli*
______6 Sam Peckinpah: **a.** *The Wild Bunch* **b.** *Straw Dogs* **c.** *Junior Bonner* **d.** *Bonnie and Clyde*
______7 King Vidor: **a.** *Track of the Cat* **b.** *Ruby Gentry* **c.** *The Fountainhead* **d.** *Northwest Passage*
______8 Mervyn LeRoy: **a.** *Mr. Skeffington* **b.** *Little Caesar* **c.** *Random Harvest* **d.** *No Time for Sergeants*
______9 Leo McCarey: **a.** *Going My Way* **b.** *The Bells of St. Mary* **c.** *Ruggles of Red Gap* **d.** *Topper*
______10 Tony Richardson: **a.** *A Taste of Honey* **b.** *Tom Jones* **c.** *The Assassination Bureau* **d.** *The Loneliness of the Long Distance Runner*

______**Score**
(5 points each)

Test 58

The Ph.D. Level

____ **1** Blake Edwards: **a.** *Lady Sings the Blues* **b.** *Days of Wine and Roses* **c.** *The Pink Panther* **d.** *The Great Race*

____ **2** Howard Hawks: **a.** *Scarface* **b.** *Bringing Up Baby* **c.** *The Big Sleep* **d.** *They Drive by Night*

____ **3** John Sturges: **a.** *The Magnificent Seven* **b.** *Gunfight at the O.K. Corral* **c.** *Vera Cruz* **d.** *The Great Escape*

____ **4** George Sidney: **a.** *The Unsinkable Molly Brown* **b.** *Kiss Me Kate* **c.** *Bye Bye Birdie* **d.** *The Harvey Girls*

____ **5** Richard Brooks: **a.** *The Blackboard Jungle* **b.** *Elmer Gantry* **c.** *Body and Soul* **d.** *In Cold Blood*

____ **6** Arthur Penn: **a.** *Little Big Man* **b.** *Hud* **c.** *Alice's Restaurant* **d.** *The Miracle Worker*

____ **7** Don Siegel: **a.** *Dirty Harry* **b.** *Paint Your Wagon* **c.** *Coogan's Bluff* **d.** *Invasion of the Body Snatchers*

____ **8** Michael Curtiz: **a.** *Mildred Pierce* **b.** *The Adventures of Robin Hood* **c.** *The Mark of Zorro* **d.** *Captain Blood*

____ **9** Lloyd Bacon: **a.** *Brother Orchid* **b.** *Give My Regards to Broadway* **c.** *Forty-Second Street* **d.** *The Enchanted Cottage*

____ **10** Lewis Milestone: **a.** *In Which We Serve* **b.** *A Walk in the Sun* **c.** *Of Mice and Men* **d.** *The Front Page*

____ **Score**
(5 points each)

Test
59

Nursery Rhymes—I Remember Mother (Goose)

Return with us now to your mother's knee and answer the following questions about children's verse.

The B.A. Level

1.____________________ What couldn't Jack Sprat do?

2.____________________ What were Jack and Jill doing up on that hill?

3.____________________ What is the destination of a cock-horse?

4.____________________ Who cut off the tails of the three blind mice?

5.____________________ Who followed Mary to school?

6.____________________ Who ran away with the spoon?

7.____________________ How many bags of wool did Baa, Baa Black Sheep have?

8.____________________ What did Tom the piper's son steal?

9.____________________ How many blackbirds were baked in a pie?

10.____________________ What did Georgie Porgie do when the boys came out to play?

__________**Score**
(5 points each)

The M.S. Level

1.____________________ How much did Jacky earn each day?

2.____________________ What did King Cole call for?

3.____________________ Who were the three men in a tub?

4.____________________ Who couldn't all the king's horses and all the king's men put together again?

5.____________________ When Daddy went-a-hunting for a baby bunting, what did he get to wrap the baby in?

6.____________________ What did the crooked man find when he walked a crooked mile?

7.____________________ What is the color of Bobby Shafto's hair?

8.____________________ Where was the little boy who looks after the sheep?

9.____________________ This old man he played eight, he played nicknack on my . . .

10.____________________ For those who don't care about hot or cold, how do they like pease pudding?

__________**Score**
(5 points each)

The Ph.D. Level

1.____________________ Who pulled Pussy out of the well?

2.____________________ What was Wee Willie Winkie wearing as he ran through town?

3.____________________ Polly put the kettle on; who took it off?

4.____________________ Where did Simple Simon fish for a whale?

5.____________________ What was the condition of Mother Hubbard's dog when she returned from the baker's?

6.____________________ What did Little Tommy Tucker get for his supper?

7.____________________ Where does the Muffin Man live?

8.____________________ What was Jack Horner eating in the corner?

9.____________________ What kind of morning was it when we went around the mulberry bush?

10.____________________ Where did Little Polly Flinders sit?

__________**Score**
(5 points each)

Test 60

The Son of Potpourri

The B.A. Level

1.________________ Who is called the Toastmaster General?

2.________________ What is the name of the Brooklyn salesman in Arthur Miller's play *Death of a Salesman?*

3.________________ What was the hit song of *The Singing Nun?*

4.________________ Who was Dr. Marcus Welby's colleague?

5.________________ What is the theme song of the Harlem Globetrotters?

6.________________ "One could do worse than be a swinger of birches" is the last line from a poem by . . .

7.________________ What was the name of the hero of J. D. Salinger's *The Catcher in the Rye?*

8.________________ Who developed the process for making rubber?

9.________________ Who was the first American to win the Nobel Peace Prize?

10.________________ *The Secret Life of Walter Mitty* concerns a . . .

__________**Score**
(5 points each)

The M.S. Level

1.________________ Who wrote the religious novel *The Robe?*

2.________________ What was the Warsaw Pact, signed in 1955?

3.________________ What marvelous discovery was made by an Arab shepherd in a cave near Qumran in 1947?

4.________________ With what radio personality do you associate: "Good evening, Mr. and Mrs. America and all the ships at sea"?

5.________________ What was the name of the world's first space passenger of Sputnik II?

6.________________ What is the name of the main square of Buenos Aires?

7.________________ What do collectors and art historians call the printed pedigree of a work of art?

8.________________ Who was Bulldog Drummond's sidekick?

9.________________ Name the rock group that recorded the hit song "Alley Oop" in the sixties?

10.________________ What is the first name of the daughter of B. O. Plenty and Gravel Gertie?

__________**Score**
(5 points each)

The Ph.D. Level

1.________________ What was the name of Captain Cook's ship on his second and third voyages?

2.________________ Who was Odysseus's wife?

3.________________ Who was the vocalist on the hit song of *Moulin Rouge?*

4.________________ What is a deltiologist?

5.________________ What was the name of the midget who pinch-hit for the St. Louis Browns in 1951?

6.________________ What was the name of the disease that killed Lou Gehrig?

7.________________ Who were the Wobblies?

8.________________ Where is the Corcoran Gallery of Art located?

9.________________ How is one's character analyzed or fortune foretold in chiromancy?

10.________________ What is the name of the world-famous Viennese stable of performing horses?

__________**Score**
(5 points each)

Test 61

Just a Song at Twilight—Love Songs

Once again you are asked to identify a familiar song from its opening words.

The B.A. Level

_____ **1** "Just a song at twilight . . ."
_____ **2** "What a day this has been . . ."
_____ **3** "Close your eyes and I'll kiss you . . ."
_____ **4** "Fish got to swim and birds got to fly . . ."
_____ **5** "When I'm calling you . . ."
_____ **6** "It's very clear . . ."
_____ **7** "The sky was blue, and high above . . ."
_____ **8** "Can it be the trees that fill the breeze . . ."
_____ **9** "Tonight you're mine completely . . ."
_____ **10** "I've been cheated, been mistreated . . ."
_____ **11** "The glow of sunset in the summer skies . . ."
_____ **12** "Once on a high and distant hill . . ."

a "All My Loving"
b "Indian Love Call"
c "Love is a Many Splendored Thing"
d "Lover, Come Back to Me"
e "Love in Bloom"
f "Will You Love Me Tomorrow"
g "When Will I Be Loved"
h "Love's Old Sweet Song"
i "Love Is Here to Stay"
j "The Things I Love"
k "Almost Like Being in Love"
l "Can't Help Loving Dat Man"

__________ **Score**
(5 points each)

The M.S. Level

_____ **1** "Not a soul down on the corner . . ."
_____ **2** "Fairy tales can come true . . ."
_____ **3** "I thought love was only true in fairy tales . . ."
_____ **4** "I used to be a rovin' lad . . ."
_____ **5** "It's not the pale moon that excites me . . ."
_____ **6** "Look at me, I'm as helpless as a kitten up a tree . . ."
_____ **7** "And I wake up in the morning with my hair down in my eyes . . ."
_____ **8** "I've just found joy . . ."
_____ **9** "Oh yeah I'll tell you something . . ."
_____ **10** "I know a dark secluded place . . ."
_____ **11** "In some secluded rendezous . . ."
_____ **12** "Daisy, Daisy, give me your answer true . . ."

a "The Nearness of You"
b "I'm a Believer"
c "Little Green Apples"
d "A Bicycle Built for Two"
e "I Want to Hold Your Hand"
f "Wedding Bells"
g "I'll Go Home with Bonnie Jean"
h "Hernando's Hideaway"
i "Cocktails for Two"
j "Young at Heart"
k "Sweet Lorraine"
l "Misty"

__________ **Score**
(5 points each)

Test 61

The Ph.D. Level

______ **1** "We were waltzing together to a dreamy melody . . ."	**a** "Leaving on a Jet Plane"
______ **2** "I listen for the whistle and I lie awake and wait . . ."	**b** "The Man That Got Away"
______ **3** "Put your sweet lips a little closer to the phone . . ."	**c** "Born to Lose"
______ **4** "I've flown around the world in a plane . . ."	**d** "Mood Indigo"
______ **5** "My bags are packed . . ."	**e** "Bali Ha'i"
______ **6** "The night is bitter . . ."	**f** "Fast Freight"
______ **7** "Do not forsake me, oh my darlin . . ."	**g** "He'll Have to Go"
______ **8** "You ain't been blue . . ."	**h** "Don't Marry Me"
______ **9** "Most people live on a lonely island . . ."	**i** "I Can't Get Started"
______ **10** "I've lived my life in vain . . ."	**j** "Changing Partners"
______ **11** "If you want to have a rosy future . . ."	**k** "Heartbreak Hotel"
______ **12** "Since my baby left me . . ."	**l** "High Noon"

__________ **Score**
(5 points each)

Test 62

Secret Identities—Quick, Find Me a Phone Booth

Superman is Clark Kent, Batman is Bruce Wayne, and Wonder Woman is Diana Prince. In this test you are required to match some "heroes" with their "real" identities.

The B.A. Level

______ **1** Chandu the Magician	**a** Captain Albright
______ **2** Super Chicken	**b** Dr. Don Blake
______ **3** Hawkgirl	**c** Frank Chandler
______ **4** Captain Midnight	**d** Kent Nelson
______ **5** The Atom	**e** Jonathon Crane
______ **6** Mighty Thor	**f** Susan Kent
______ **7** Scarecrow	**g** Henry Cabot Henhouse III
______ **8** Bulletgirl	**h** Dr. Henry Pym
______ **9** Ant Man	**i** Al Pratt
______ **10** Dr. Fate	**j** Shiera Sanders

__________ **Score**
(5 points each)

The M.S. Level

______ **1** Marvelman	**a** Roy Harper
______ **2** Speedy	**b** Richard Stanton
______ **3** Trickster	**c** Wesley Dodds
______ **4** Doll Girl	**d** Mickey Moran
______ **5** Captain Future	**e** Lar Gand
______ **6** Sandman	**f** Ben Grimm
______ **7** The Thing	**g** Martha Roberts
______ **8** Black Cat	**h** Curtis Newton
______ **9** Madam Fatal	**i** James Jesse
______ **10** Mon-El	**j** Linda Turner

__________ **Score**
(5 points each)

The Ph.D. Level

______ **1** The Shield	**a** George Chance
______ **2** The Beast	**b** Wally West
______ **3** The Ghost	**c** Harvey Hudson
______ **4** Whizzer	**d** Hank McCoy
______ **5** Firefly	**e** Len Smart
______ **6** The Falcon	**f** Joe Higgins
______ **7** Captain Cold	**g** John Aman
______ **8** Iceman	**h** Bob Frank
______ **9** Amazing Man	**i** Sam Wilson
______ **10** Kid Flash	**j** Bobby Drake

__________ **Score**
(5 points each)

Test 63

Double Features—Saturday Afternoon's Delight—A Reprise

Match the dream double features with the movie stars who appeared in them.

The B.A. Level

______ **1** *Command Decision* and *Mogambo*	**a** Jane Fonda
______ **2** *Beat the Devil* and *Trapeze*	**b** Ava Gardner
______ **3** *The Inn of the Sixth Happiness* and *Notorious*	**c** Maureen O'Hara
______ **4** *Young Man With a Horn* and *Lust for Life*	**d** Jennifer Jones
______ **5** *The Quiet Man* and *Mr. Hobbs Takes a Vacation*	**e** Clark Gable
______ **6** *Gypsy* and *On the Waterfront*	**f** Gene Kelly
______ **7** *The Little Hut* and *King Solomon's Mines*	**g** Gina Lollobrigida
______ **8** *The Pirate* and *Marjorie Morningstar*	**h** Louis Jourdan
______ **9** *Any Wednesday* and *Barefoot in the Park*	**i** Karl Malden
______ **10** *Portrait of Jennie* and *Good Morning Miss Dove*	**j** Stewart Granger
______ **11** *Bhawani Junction* and *The Night of the Iguana*	**k** Kirk Douglas
______ **12** *Gigi* and *Can-Can*	**l** Ingrid Bergman

__________ **Score**
(5 points each)

The M.S. Level

______ **1** *Myra Breckinridge* and *My Little Chickadee*	**a** Virginia Mayo
______ **2** *The Purple Heart* and *Laura*	**b** Joan Collins
______ **3** *Hans Christian Andersen* and *The Five Pennies*	**c** Peter Boyle
______ **4** *Critic's Choice* and *Yours, Mine and Ours*	**d** Raymond Massey
______ **5** *Road to Hong Kong* and *Rally Round the Flag Boys*	**e** Joanne Woodward
______ **6** *Joe* and *The Friends of Eddie Coyle*	**f** Mae West
______ **7** *Battleground* and *The Caine Mutiny*	**g** Dana Andrews
______ **8** *Hitler* and *Moby Dick*	**h** Judy Garland
______ **9** *The Fugitive Kind* and *A Big Hand for the Little Lady*	**i** Richard Basehart
______ **10** *Summer Stock* and *The Clock*	**j** Danny Kaye
______ **11** *East of Eden* and *Abe Lincoln in Illinois*	**k** Van Johnson
______ **12** *Up in Arms* and *Captain Horatio Hornblower*	**l** Lucille Ball

__________ **Score**
(5 points each)

Test 63

The Ph.D. Level

____ **1** *Shane* and *Panic in the Streets*	**a** Richard Egan
____ **2** *A Man for All Seasons* and *Major Barbara*	**b** Ronald Reagan
____ **3** *They Drive by Night* and *Roadhouse*	**c** Peter Ustinov
____ **4** *Dark Victory* and *King's Row*	**d** Joan Blondell
____ **5** *Oklahoma!* and *The Illustrated Man*	**e** Celeste Holm
____ **6** *The 300 Spartans* and *The View from Pompey's Head*	**f** Irene Dunne
____ **7** *A Tree Grows in Brooklyn* and *Footlight Parade*	**g** Ida Lupino
____ **8** *The Sea Wolf* and *The Stranger*	**h** Jack Palance
____ **9** *I Married a Witch* and *This Gun for Hire*	**i** Wendy Hiller
____ **10** *Come to the Stable* and *The Tender Trap*	**j** Veronica Lake
____ **11** *Viva Max* and *Romanoff and Juliet*	**k** Edward G. Robinson
____ **12** *The Awful Truth* and *The Mudlark*	**l** Rod Steiger

________ **Score**
(5 points each)

Test
64

I Remember Them Well—Movie Stars

In this test, you are to identify an actor or actress from the clues that suggest two of his or her movie roles.

The B.A. Level

1.________________ She was convinced she was ugly until Burt Lancaster came along, and she proved a match for an efficiency expert.

2.________________ He was a limping gangster who loved Doris Day, and he sold Coke in Berlin.

3.________________ He was a wine expert with Goldie Hawn as mistress, and he went from a gardener to a presidential adviser.

4.________________ She was to give one last kiss to a rock star, and she recreated a Claire Trevor role in a remake of a John Wayne classic.

5.________________ She parachuted into Peter O'Toole's automobile, and she collected shells at Crab Key.

6.________________ He was a wimpy Fletcher Christian, and he was a Mexican revolutionary.

7.________________ He was an insurance investigator who could smell fraud, and he tracked down Orson Welles.

8.________________ He committed suicide in his senate office, and he was a hoodlum priest.

9.________________ He proved he couldn't sing in No Name City, and he was famous as the man with no name.

10.________________ She tried to convince Gregory Peck that he would live at Kilimanjaro, and she was Andrew Jackson's wife.

__________**Score (5 points each)**

The M.S. Level

1.________________ He once played Billy the Kid, and he was a con man with Robert Redford.

2.________________ He didn't have to say he was sorry, and he was outacted by his daughter.

3.________________ He had ambitions to be President of the U.S., and he lost an election to be mayor of a major city.

4.________________ James Mason loved her daughter and not her, and her swimming abilities saved others although they were fatal for her.

5.________________ She pleaded for Kirk Douglas's understanding, and she kept Frank Sinatra by making him feel guilty.

6.________________ She could have climbed every mountain, and she was the long-suffering wife of Max Von Sydow.

7.________________ Her words and music were "thou swell," and she was the wife of Glenn Miller.

8.________________ He learned how to cheat from Bobby Morse, and he tried to get the U.S. to take advantage of an accidental attack on Moscow.

9.________________ He enjoyed renting his apartments to luscious young women, and he tried to help his neighbor inherit millions.

10.________________ She was a Russian pilot romanced by John Wayne, and she loved Houdini.

__________**Score (5 points each)**

The Ph.D. Level

1.________________ He married, divorced and remarried Debbie Reynolds, and he played a silent screen comedian.

2.________________ He was Mr. Scratch, and he was the unsuspecting accomplice of the murder in a version of an Agatha Christie movie.

3.________________ She was defended by Katharine Hepburn, and she rang Dean Martin's bells.

4.________________ She loved Sir Boss, and she was pursued by Jeff Chandler.

5.________________ She answered to a whistle, and she didn't want to fall in love with Cameron Mitchell.

6.________________ He led the L.A. Rams to a championship, and he liked Jack Warden's taste in women.

7.________________ She helped kill Walter Slezak, and she was Catherine the Great.

8.________________ He made devilish prescriptions for Mia Farrow, and he defended General Billy Mitchell.

9.________________ He tried to share a pillow with Doris Day, and he took advantage of his position as a counselor in a high school.

10.________________ She was Marcellius's love, and she was a religious leader who had a thing for Burt Lancaster.

__________**Score (5 points each)**

Test 65

Miscellaneous TV Trivia

The B.A. Level

1.________________ Who played Granny on *The Beverly Hillbillies?*

2.________________ Who is famous for his character Joe the Bartender?

3.________________ Who frequently delivered the line "Mother always liked you best"?

4.________________ Who was the "Sock it to me" girl?

5.________________ Who created the character Maude Frickett?

6.________________ Who played Charley Weaver?

7.________________ Who played the young Kunta Kinte in *Roots?*

8.________________ Maude was a spin-off of what successful TV show?

9.________________ What role did Cloris Leachman create in *The Mary Tyler Moore Show?*

10.________________ What TV program is introduced by the words ". . . the thrill of victory, the agony of defeat"?

11.________________ What Oscar winning actress played Hazel?

12.________________ Who did the voices of Bert and Harry Piel?

__________**Score**
(5 points each)

The M.S. Level

1.________________ Who played Marlo Thomas's boyfriend on *That Girl?*

2.________________ Who played Endora, Samantha's mother, on *Bewitched?*

3.________________ Who was Lucille Ball's male co-star in *The Lucy Show?*

4.________________ What role did Bob Denver play on *The Many Loves of Dobie Gillis?*

5.________________ What number was Patrick McGoohan in *The Prisoner?*

6.________________ What was the name of Baretta's pet?

7.________________ What role did Mary Kay Place play on *Mary Hartman, Mary Hartman?*

8.________________ What was the first prime time cartoon series?

9.________________ Who was the host of *Omnibus?*

10.________________ Who was Fred Gwynne's partner on *Car 54, Where Are You?*

11.________________ Who played the navigator Mr. Sulu on *Star Trek?*

12.________________ What TV series featured Hedda Hopper's son and in what role?

__________**Score**
(5 points each)

The Ph.D. Level

1.________________ Who played "the girl in the bathtub" on *The Ernie Kovacs Show?*

2.________________ Who was the statuesque robot on *My Living Doll?*

3.________________ What role did Geraldine Page win an Emmy for in Truman Capote's *A Christmas Memory?*

4.________________ Who played Bruce Wayne's butler Alfred?

5.________________ What were Mia Farrow and Ryan O'Neal's roles on *Peyton Place?*

6.________________ What was the name of the secret agent played by Patrick McGoohan?

7.________________ What was the name of the unsuccessful American series fashioned after *Upstairs, Downstairs?*

8.________________ Who was the star of an NBC-TV film entitled *The Law?*

9.________________ Who played the oldest son when *My Three Sons* began?

10.________________ Who was Walter Cronkite's predecessor on CBS's evening news?

11.________________ Who were the regulars on *The Garry Moore Show?*

12.________________ Who were the stars of *Love Among the Ruins?*

__________**Score**
(5 points each)

Test 66

Detectives of Fiction—Clue Me In

Are you a mystery fan? If so, you should have little difficulty in matching these famous detectives and their creators.

The B.A. Level

______1	Bertha Cool	**a**	John D. MacDonald
______2	Parker Pyne	**b**	Victor Hugo
______3	Travis McGee	**c**	Dan J. Marlowe
______4	Arsène Lupin	**d**	A. A. Fair
______5	Shell Scott	**e**	Louis Joseph Vance
______6	Rick Holman	**f**	Richard S. Prather
______7	Michael Lanyard (The Lone Wolf)	**g**	Carter Brown
______8	Drake	**h**	John Dickson Carr
______9	Dr. Gideon Fell	**i**	Maurice Leblanc
______10	Inspector Javert	**j**	Agatha Christie

____________**Score**
(5 points each)

The M.S. Level

______1	Deputy Parr	**a**	Melville Davisson Post
______2	Max Carrados	**b**	Edward S. Aarons
______3	Sam Durell	**c**	John Dickson Carr
______4	Uncle Abner	**d**	Manning Coles
______5	Colonel March	**e**	Wilkie Collins
______6	Reggie Fortune	**f**	John Creasey
______7	Barney Cook	**g**	Frederick Irving Anderson
______8	Tommy Hambledon	**h**	Harvey O'Higgins
______9	Sergeant Cuff	**i**	Henry Christopher Bailey
______10	Dr. Palfrey	**j**	Ernest Bramah

____________**Score**
(5 points each)

The Ph.D. Level

______1	John J. Malone	**a**	John Dickson Carr
______2	Mr. Pinderton	**b**	Craig Rice
______3	The Toff	**c**	Judson Philips
______4	John Putnam Thatcher	**d**	Kenneth Robeson
______5	Sir Henry Merrivale	**e**	Arthur B. Reeve
______6	Asey Mayo	**f**	David Frome
______7	Richard Henry Benson	**g**	Emma Lathen
______8	Craig Kennedy	**h**	John Creasey
______9	Mark Bolan	**i**	Phoebe Atwood Taylor
______10	Peter Styles	**j**	Don Pendleton

____________**Score**
(5 points each)

Test 67

For a Few Points—A Reprise

Answer the following questions and take the points.

The B.A. Level

1. For three points name the actors who play the comedy writers for Alan Brady played by Carl Reiner on television.
2. For five points name the shapes of the breakfast cereal Lucky Charms.
3. For twelve points name the signs of the zodiac.
4. For three points name the actors who played the retired Texas Rangers in *The Over-the-Hill Gang*.
5. For three points name Daisy Duck's nieces.
6. For three points name the standard units of measure of the metric system.
7. For five points name the types of quadrilaterals.
8. For five points name the states of the original thirteen that were named after real persons.
9. For four points name the four most populous countries.
10. For three points give the first names of the baseball-playing DiMaggio brothers.

___________**Score**

The M.S. Level

1. For three points name the daughters of Phorcys and Ceto in Greek mythology.
2. For nine points name the colors of the solid-colored pool balls.
3. For four points name the actors on the TV series *Leave It to Beaver*.
4. For two points give the first names of the Chevrolet brothers.
5. For nine points name the movies in which Spencer Tracy and Katharine Hepburn co-starred.
6. For six points name the John Jakes American Bicentennial novel series.
7. For five points name the main characters of the *Perry Mason* TV series.
8. For two points name *Star Trek*'s Mr. Spock's parents' first names.
9. For ten points name the plagues of Egypt.

___________**Score**

The Ph.D. Level

1. For four points name the conspirators who were hanged after the assassination of Abraham Lincoln.
2. For twelve points list what a Scout is.
3. For eight points name the "Black Sox" players who were banned from baseball.
4. For two points name the Brothers Grimm.
5. For five points name the Hall of Famers Carl Hubbell struck out in succession in the 1934 all-star game.
6. For four points give the first names of the husbands of Maude.
7. For five points name the Platonic solids.
8. For five points give the first names of the characters in the dramatic-comedy series *The Goldbergs*.
9. For two points name the radio vocal duo the Happiness Boys.
10. For three points name the original panelists of the radio quiz program *Information, Please*.

___________**Score**

Test 68

Broadway Musicals—Of Thee I Sing

The most American of entertainment is the Broadway musical. Surely you can easily match the following songs with the musical in which it was featured.

The B.A. Level

______**1** "I Could Have Danced All Night"	**a** *The Sound of Music*
______**2** "I'm in Love with a Wonderful Guy"	**b** *The Student Prince*
______**3** "Before the Parade Passes By"	**c** *Damn Yankees*
______**4** "My Favorite Things"	**d** *Gentlemen Prefer Blondes*
______**5** "Don't Rain on My Parade"	**e** *South Pacific*
______**6** "Heart"	**f** *West Side Story*
______**7** "A Little Girl from Little Rock"	**g** *The Most Happy Fella*
______**8** "A Boy Like That"	**h** *My Fair Lady*
______**9** "If Momma Was Married"	**i** *Hello, Dolly!*
______**10** "Standing on the Corner"	**j** *Call Me Madam*
______**11** "You're Just in Love"	**k** *Funny Girl*
______**12** "Golden Days"	**l** *Gypsy*

__________**Score**
(5 points each)

The M.S. Level

______**1** "Out of My Dreams"	**a** *A Funny Thing Happened on the Way to the Forum*
______**2** "Do You Love Me?"	**b** *Carousel*
______**3** "I Believe in You"	**c** *Kiss Me, Kate*
______**4** "Goodnight, My Someone"	**d** *Guys and Dolls*
______**5** "We Kiss in a Shadow"	**e** *Oklahoma!*
______**6** "A Bushel and a Peck"	**f** *Man of La Mancha*
______**7** "Where is the Life that Late I Led?"	**g** *How to Succeed in Business Without Really Trying*
______**8** "Hey, There"	**h** *The King and I*
______**9** "I'm Only Thinking of Him"	**i** *Fiddler on the Roof*
______**10** "Comedy Tonight"	**j** *Camelot*
______**11** "What's the Use of Wond'rin'"	**k** *The Music Man*
______**12** "Follow Me"	**l** *Pajama Game*

__________**Score**
(5 points each)

WILLIAM MORROW AND COMPANY, INC.
QUILL
FIELDING PUBLICATIONS
105 MADISON AVENUE
NEW YORK, NEW YORK 10016

Test 68

The Ph.D. Level

______ **1** "The Girl That I Marry"	**a** *Mame*
______ **2** "Just in Time"	**b** *La Plume de Ma Tante*
______ **3** "It's All Right With Me"	**c** *Annie Get Your Gun*
______ **4** "Restless Heart"	**d** *Song of Norway*
______ **5** "Where Are You?"	**e** *High Button Shoes*
______ **6** "Strange Music"	**f** *Carnival*
______ **7** "Precision"	**g** *Bells Are Ringing*
______ **8** "Gooch's Song"	**h** *Follow the Girls*
______ **9** "Little Tin Box"	**i** *Can-Can*
______ **10** "South America, Take it Away"	**j** *Fanny*
______ **11** "I Still Get Jealous"	**k** *Call Me Mister*
______ **12** "Her Face"	**l** *Fiorello!*

__________ **Score**
(5 points each)

Test 69

Authors and Their Works—And Then I Wrote

In this test you are to show your literary knowledge by finding two works of the given authors or playwrights.

The B.A. Level

_____ **1** Truman Capote
_____ **2** Robert Bolt
_____ **3** James Jones
_____ **4** John Osborne
_____ **5** Graham Greene
_____ **6** Ayn Rand
_____ **7** James T. Farrell
_____ **8** Irving Wallace
_____ **9** Arthur Miller
_____ **10** John O'Hara

a *The Pistol*
b *Atlas Shrugged*
c *Studs Lonigan A Trilogy*
d *A View from the Bridge*
e *In Cold Blood*
f *Appointment in Samarra*
g *The Fountainhead*
h *The Entertainer*
i *The Heart of the Matter*
j *Breakfast at Tiffany's*
k *Look Back in Anger*
l *The Chapman Report*
m *Flowering Cherry*
n *The Prize*
o *The Power and the Glory*
p *A Man for All Seasons*
q *Some Came Running*
r *After the Fall*
s *A World I Never Made*
t *Butterfield 8*

__________ **Score**
(5 points each)

The M.S. Level

_____ **1** Daphne du Maurier
_____ **2** Samuel Beckett
_____ **3** Ken Kesey
_____ **4** John Updike
_____ **5** Henry Miller
_____ **6** Norman Mailer
_____ **7** Sylvia Plath
_____ **8** Carson McCullers
_____ **9** Tennessee Williams
_____ **10** Pearl Buck

a *The Centaur*
b *Saturn Never Sleeps*
c *Ariel*
d *The Night of the Iguana*
e *One Flew Over the Cuckoo's Nest*
f *Rabbit Run*
g *Rebecca*
h *The Bell Jar*
i *Endgame*
j *Dragon Seed*
k *The Rose Tattoo*
l *Frenchman's Creek*
m *The Deer Park*
n *Member of the Wedding*
o *Tropic of Cancer*
p *Waiting for Godot*
q *The Heart is a Lonely Hunter*
r *Quiet Days in Clichy*
s *An American Dream*
t *Sometimes a Great Notion*

__________ **Score**
(5 points each)

The Ph.D. Level

_____ **1** Erskine Caldwell
_____ **2** Eugene Ionesco
_____ **3** Gore Vidal
_____ **4** Noel Coward
_____ **5** Peter De Vries
_____ **6** Shirley Jackson
_____ **7** Ray Bradbury
_____ **8** Katherine Anne Porter
_____ **9** William Saroyan
_____ **10** Anais Nin

a *The Best Man*
b *The Novel of the Future*
c *The Illustrated Man*
d *Rhinoceros*
e *The Four-Chambered Heart*
f *God's Little Acre*
g *Ship of Fools*
h *Quadrille*
i *Claudelle Inglish*
j *Visit to a Small Planet*
k *Comfort Me with Apples*
l *The Tunnel of Love*
m *Life among the Savages*
n *Pale Horse, Pale Rider*
o *The Killer*
p *The Cave Dwellers*
q *The Martian Chronicles*
r *The Haunting of Hill House*
s *Present Laughter*
t *The Time of Your Life*

__________ **Score**
(5 points each)

Test 70

Still More Potpourri

The B.A. Level

1.________________ Where is the home of the Wizard of Oz?

2.________________ What was the name of Franklin D. Roosevelt's Scottie dog?

3.________________ What was the name of the skunk in the Disney movie *Bambi*?

4.________________ What newspaper showed the election night headline "Dewey Defeats Truman"?

5.________________ What was Kunta Kinte's slave name in *Roots*?

6.________________ The initials ICBM refer to . . .

7.________________ What famous painting of Leonardo da Vinci's did France send on a visit to the U.S. in the early sixties?

8.________________ During World War II, the OPA was an important Washington agency. Name it.

9.________________ Who was known as the Little Flower?

10.________________ Who was slain by David?

__________**Score**
(5 points each)

The M.S. Level

1.________________ What is the name of Samantha and Darren Stephen's daughter in *Bewitched*?

2.________________ Who was the Cleveland Indians' second baseman who performed the only unassisted triple play in World Series history?

3.________________ What mountains separate Asia from Europe?

4.________________ Who was the arch-enemy of Dudley Do-Right?

5.________________ Who killed Cock Robin?

6.________________ The popular singer Pat Boone is the author of a book entitled . . . ?

7.________________ What is Gresham's law?

8.________________ What is the name of the B-17 to which the misfits were assigned in *Twelve O'Clock High*?

9.________________ Who was the first Secretary-General of the U.N.?

10.________________ Who sponsored the radio program *Edgar Bergen and Charlie McCarthy*?

__________**Score**
(5 points each)

The Ph.D. Level

1.________________ Whose portrait appears on a $1,000 bill?

2.________________ What is rock singer Alice Cooper's real name?

3.________________ What was the favorite song of Katharine Hepburn's pet leopard in the movie *Bringing Up Baby*?

4.________________ What is the oldest food franchise in the U.S.?

5.________________ What was the title of Billy Rose's newspaper column?

6.________________ Who was the victim of Nathan F. Leopold, Jr. and Richard A. Loeb?

7.________________ Chaucer's poem in which a group gathers on St. Valentine's Day to select their mates is . . .

8.________________ Who was the American publisher, founder of *Reader's Digest*?

9.________________ Who was Chingachgook's son in *The Last of the Mohicans*?

10.________________ What is absolute zero?

__________**Score**
(5 points each)

Test 71

The Name's the Same—Movie Stars

Although many actors and actresses change their names, many notable performers share the same last name. Identify the pairs of "stars" from the following clues.

The B.A. Level

1.____________________ He was "the great profile". His sister played crotchety old ladies usually with hearts of gold.

2.____________________ He is a Swedish writer-director. She is a Swedish leading actress.

3.____________________ He was Batman. She was a little chickadee?

4.____________________ She was best as Georgy Girl. Her sister is as well known for her espousal of causes as for her acting.

5.____________________ He was America's most decorated soldier. He left the screen for politics and the Senate.

6.____________________ She was a stunningly talented child actress. He was Knute Rockne.

7.____________________ She starred for Howard Hughes in *The Outlaw*. She was very successful in the thirties and forties as a career woman.

8.____________________ He is the star of M.A.S.H. His father was George Gershwin.

9.____________________ His mistress was Judy Holliday. She was saved and then assaulted by Walter Huston.

10.____________________ She was Anna who danced with a king. He wanted to find his own special island.

__________**Score**
(5 points each)

The M.S. Level

1.____________________ She was killed in a shower. She was raped by Stanley.

2.____________________ He danced and sang in the rain. She became a real life princess.

3.____________________ She was Cricket. He was Gunn.

4.____________________ He was a novelist who wrote mainly about sex in suburbia. She was John Wayne's leading lady in many enjoyable movies.

5.____________________ She projected a scatterbrained wife for 30 years. He was Benny Goodman.

6.____________________ He founded the Actor's Studio. His daughter was Kim Novak's sister in *Picnic*.

7.____________________ She didn't know anything about "birthing babies." He usually played tough, sexy, and determined men.

8.____________________ He made several Disney movies. She won an Academy Award as Bernadette.

9.____________________ Her stardom nearly rivals that of her mother. Her father directed many fine musicals.

10.____________________ He portrayed Dennis the Menace on TV. She is a former dancer who made several forgettable movies.

__________**Score**
(5 points each)

The Ph.D. Level

1.____________________ She is a beautiful blonde and a leading socialite. His best role was as Bette Davis's fiancé.

2.____________________ He was a wizard. She was a cafe singer portrayed in a biopic by Ann Blyth.

3.____________________ He made many movies but became a TV star by knowing best. He was a Uriah Heep you could really detest.

4.____________________ He is at his best in sinister or horrific parts. She had her early life glamorized in a movie in which her mother was the central character.

5.____________________ He was killed at the Sierra Madre. She was the mother of the bride.

6.____________________ He admired gorillas and Marx. He was Lord Melbourne in *Victoria the Great*.

7.____________________ He is usually seen as a nervous cigar-chewing character. She was the queen of the silent serials.

8.____________________ She was Fiona's younger sister. He has a slow drawl and gangly walk.

9.____________________ He married Mary Pickford. She danced with Fred Astaire.

10.____________________ He talked to a mule. She was a sharp-featured character actress.

__________**Score**
(5 points each)

Test 72

Famous Quotations II—Who Said That?

The B.A. Level

_____ **1** "I am as strong as a bull moose and you can use me to the limit."
_____ **2** "If you can't stand the heat, get out of the kitchen."
_____ **3** "Virtue is its own reward."
_____ **4** "Genius is one percent inspiration and ninety-nine percent perspiration."
_____ **5** "I have seen war . . . I hate war."
_____ **6** "Rose is a rose is a rose is a rose."
_____ **7** "A verbal contract isn't worth the paper it's written on."
_____ **8** "I teach you the Superman. Man is something that is to be surpassed."
_____ **9** "Always do right. This will gratify some people and astonish the rest."
_____ **10** "As long as I count the votes, what are you going to do about it?"

a Harry S Truman
b Franklin D. Roosevelt
c William Marcy Tweed
d Mark Twain
e Samuel Goldwyn
f Theodore Roosevelt
g Thomas Alva Edison
h Friedrich Wilhelm Nietzsche
i Gertrude Stein
j John Dryden

_____ **Score**
(5 points each)

The M.S. Level

_____ **1** "Any man more right than his neighbor constitutes a majority of one."
_____ **2** "I believe that man will not merely endure; he will prevail."
_____ **3** "Certain women should be struck regularly, like gongs."
_____ **4** "But it does move."
_____ **5** "Give me where to stand and I will move the earth."
_____ **6** "A doctor can bury his mistakes but an architect can only advise his clients to plant vines."
_____ **7** "Growing old isn't so bad when you consider the alternative."
_____ **8** "It took me fifteen years to discover I had no talent for writing, but I couldn't give it up because by that time I was too famous."
_____ **9** "If at first you don't succeed, try, try again. Then quit. There's no use being a damn fool about it."
_____ **10** "Man—a creature made at the end of the week's work when God was tired."

a Galileo Galilei
b Mark Twain
c Henry David Thoreau
d Maurice Chevalier
e Frank Lloyd Wright
f Robert Benchley
g W. C. Fields
h William Faulkner
i Noel Coward
j Archimedes

_____ **Score**
(5 points each)

Test 72

The Ph.D. Level

______ **1** "Philosophy is a systematic reflection upon the common experience of mankind."
______ **2** "Conservatives are not necessarily stupid, but most stupid people are conservatives."
______ **3** "A liberal is a man who leaves the room when the fight begins."
______ **4** "I shall never believe that God plays dice with the world."
______ **5** "Mathematics is the science which draws necessary conclusions."
______ **6** "God made integers, all else is the work of man."
______ **7** "I propose to fight it out on this line if it takes all summer."
______ **8** "Physics is experience, arranged in economical order."
______ **9** "My center is giving way, my right is pushed back, situation excellent, I am attacking."
______ **10** "Outside the kingdom of the Lord there is no nation which is greater than any other. God and history will remember your judgment."

a Heywood Broun
b Ulysses S. Grant
c Ferdinand Foch
d Benjamin Peirce
e Robert Maynard Hutchins
f Haile Selassie
g John Stuart Mill
h Leopold Kronecker
i Ernst Mach
j Albert Einstein

__________ **Score**
(5 points each)

Test 73

More Double Features

Once again you are to match movie stars with a double feature of their films.

The B.A. Level

______**1** *Tea and Sympathy* and *Beloved Infidel*	**a** Shirley MacLaine
______**2** *Under the Yum Yum Tree* and *The Out of Towners*	**b** Orson Welles
______**3** *The Killers* and *Cat Ballou*	**c** Betty Grable
______**4** *Sweet Charity* and *My Geisha*	**d** Jane Wyman
______**5** *Hombre* and *Judge Roy Bean*	**e** Lee Marvin
______**6** *Gentleman Jim* and *Virginia City*	**f** Deborah Kerr
______**7** *Mother Wore Tights* and *Tin Pan Alley*	**g** Katharine Hepburn
______**8** *Pat and Mike* and *The Lion in Winter*	**h** Rex Harrison
______**9** *Midnight Lace* and *The Fourposter*	**i** Jack Lemmon
______**10** *The Third Man* and *A Man for All Seasons*	**j** Julie Christie
______**11** *Pollyanna* and *The Lost Weekend*	**k** Errol Flynn
______**12** *Billy Liar* and *McCabe and Mrs. Miller*	**l** Paul Newman

__________**Score**
(5 points each)

The M.S. Level

______**1** *The Misfits* and *The Young Lions*	**a** Marlon Brando
______**2** *Forty Pounds of Trouble* and *The Boston Strangler*	**b** Anne Baxter
______**3** *A Letter to Three Wives* and *Forever Amber*	**c** Rosalind Russell
______**4** *Come Fill the Cup* and *Man of a Thousand Faces*	**d** Lana Turner
______**5** *A Walk on the Wild Side* and *The Razor's Edge*	**e** Linda Darnell
______**6** *The Poseidon Adventure* and *McHale's Navy*	**f** Bing Crosby
______**7** *The Wild One* and *The Ugly American*	**g** Tony Curtis
______**8** *Holiday Inn* and *High Society*	**h** Cyd Charisse
______**9** *Brigadoon* and *Two Weeks in Another Town*	**i** Jean Simmons
______**10** *Imitation of Life* and *The Merry Widow*	**j** Montgomery Clift
______**11** *Sister Kenny* and *Auntie Mame*	**k** James Cagney
______**12** *Great Expectations* and *The Actress*	**l** Ernest Borgnine

__________**Score**
(5 points each)

Test 73

The Ph.D. Level

_____ **1** *Billy Budd* and *Her Twelve Men*	**a** Shirley Temple
_____ **2** *Gung Ho* and *Last of the Mohicans*	**b** Jean Hagen
_____ **3** *Angels With Dirty Faces* and *The Man Who Came to Dinner*	**c** Fred MacMurray
_____ **4** *All the Brothers Were Valiant* and *A Yank at Oxford*	**d** Gene Tierney
_____ **5** *Fort Apache* and *Wee Willie Winkie*	**e** Thomas Mitchell
_____ **6** *Old Acquaintance* and *Becky Sharp*	**f** Rita Hayworth
_____ **7** *Alias Nick Beal* and *The Hunchback of Notre Dame*	**g** Robert Ryan
_____ **8** *Adam's Rib* and *Carbine Williams*	**h** Ann Sheridan
_____ **9** *If I Were King* and *We're No Angels*	**i** Miriam Hopkins
_____ **10** *Heaven Can Wait* and *Belle Starr*	**j** Robert Taylor
_____ **11** *The Strawberry Blonde* and *They Came to Corduro*	**k** Basil Rathbone
_____ **12** *Pushover* and *Kisses for My President*	**l** Randolph Scott

__________ **Score**
(5 points each)

Test 74

Grammy Awards—Sing, Sing, Sing

Now if I was a disk jockey I'd tell you how groovy it would be if you could match each of the award winning disks in this test with the cool cats who made them. Or perhaps that message is a bit outdated. Oh well, proceed anyway.

The B.A. Level

____**1** "I Honestly Love You"	**a** Stevie Wonder
____**2** "Black Moses"	**b** Helen Reddy
____**3** "Up, Up and Away"	**c** Bobby Gentry
____**4** "Mack the Knife"	**d** Olivia Newton-John
____**5** "Bridge Over Troubled Water"	**e** Ray Charles
____**6** "You Are the Sunshine of My Life"	**f** Bobby Darin
____**7** "Catch a Falling Star"	**g** Dionne Warwick
____**8** "I Am Woman"	**h** Isaac Hayes
____**9** "Strangers in the Night"	**i** Perry Como
____**10** "Georgia on My Mind"	**j** 5th Dimension
____**11** "Ode to Billy Joe"	**k** Simon and Garfunkel
____**12** "Do You Know the Way to San Jose?"	**l** Frank Sinatra

________**Score**
(5 points each)

The M.S. Level

____**1** "Everybody's Talkin'"	**a** James Taylor
____**2** "Evergreen"	**b** Domenico Modugno
____**3** "Pink Panther"	**c** The Captain and Tennille
____**4** "A Taste of Honey"	**d** Harry Nilsson
____**5** "Love Will Keep Us Together"	**e** Henry Mancini
____**6** "Killing Me Softly With His Song"	**f** Jack Jones
____**7** "Tequila"	**g** Herb Alpert and The Tijuana Brass
____**8** "You've Got a Friend"	**h** Roberta Flack
____**9** "Everything Is Beautiful"	**i** Jose Feliciano
____**10** "Light My Fire"	**j** Barbra Streisand
____**11** "Lollipops and Roses"	**k** The Champs
____**12** "Volare"	**l** Ray Stevens

________**Score**
(5 points each)

The Ph.D. Level

____ **1** "Smackwater Jack"	**a** Al Hirt
____ **2** "Hotel California"	**b** Quincy Jones
____ **3** "The Entertainer"	**c** Linda Ronstadt
____ **4** "It's Too Late"	**d** Ella Fitzgerald
____ **5** "Hasten Down the Wind"	**e** Mason Williams
____ **6** "But Not for Me"	**f** Marvin Hamlisch
____ **7** "Classical Gas"	**g** George Benson
____ **8** "Is That All There Is?"	**h** The Eagles
____ **9** "Breezin'"	**i** Janis Ian
____ **10** "Java"	**j** Carole King
____ **11** "At Seventeen"	**k** Eydie Gorme
____ **12** "If He Walked Into My Life"	**l** Peggy Lee

________ **Score**
(5 points each)

Test 75

Psychology—You're All Right, How Am I?

No college education is complete without a superficial knowledge of psychology. You can prove your mettle by matching the terms that have become a part of our everyday conversation with the nearly correct definitions.

The B.A. Level

_____ **1** a tendency to display the genitalia for the purpose of inducing personal sexual excitement and satisfaction
_____ **2** a process whereby an individual is affected by a radical change in beliefs through intensive indoctrination
_____ **3** an abnormal sexual desire characterized by pleasure derived by suffering physical pain either at one's own hand or others
_____ **4** a personality disorder that is not totally incapacitating
_____ **5** the emotional attachment of a child for the opposite sexed parent
_____ **6** an emotional disorder characterized by dissociation, as indicated by such symptoms as amnesia, paralysis, anesthesia, etc.
_____ **7** a sex deviation in which the individual derives sexual pleasure from watching the erotic behavior of others
_____ **8** sexual contacts, especially intercourse, between a human being and an animal
_____ **9** a persistent neurotic impulse to steal, particularly without an economic motive or need
_____ **10** the false perception of a sensory nature

a brainwashing
b neurosis
c hysteria
d hallucination
e voyeurism
f exhibitionism
g kleptomania
h bestiality
i masochism
j Oedipus complex

_____ **Score**
(5 points each)

The M.S. Level

_____ **1** refers to the self; the individual as aware of himself
_____ **2** a pathological condition characterized by an erotic preoccupation with certain parts of the body or with certain articles of clothing
_____ **3** a type of self-analysis where one looks within his own mind
_____ **4** a retreat to an earlier, and usually less adequate, mode of response
_____ **5** a form of mental illness characterized by extreme "withdrawal from reality"
_____ **6** an extreme, and usually pathological, dread of some specific type of situation or stimulation in the absence of any "realistic" danger
_____ **7** a type of personality in which one's own interests are directed mainly toward external and social factors
_____ **8** the habit, or behavior, of dressing in clothes of the opposite sex
_____ **9** an extreme or exaggerated desire on the part of a human male for sexual participation and satisfaction
_____ **10** a form of mental derangement in which the individual has an irresistible and persistent desire to set fires

a introspection
b schizophrenia
c pyromania
d fetishism
e transvestism
f satyriasis
g ego
h extrovert
i phobia
j regression

_____ **Score**
(5 points each)

Test 75

The Ph.D. Level

_____ **1** a type of neurosis that is characterized by marked anxiety and rigidity of thinking

_____ **2** the individual who has both male and female reproductive organs in the body

_____ **3** the opinion and belief by an individual that his culture and group are superior to other cultures and groups

_____ **4** a type of behavior in which the individual excessively overestimates his abilities and self-importance

_____ **5** the denial of the knowledge of all existence and or existence itself

_____ **6** the study of the science of reality or existence

_____ **7** a mentally subnormal individual who has unusual ability in one or more specialized activities

_____ **8** the lack of ability to concentrate or to maintain attention

_____ **9** a lessening of anxiety or fear and other feelings of guilt, inferiority, or depression by allowing the individual to relive traumatic and troublesome past experiences through a permissive "self-expression" of them

_____ **10** a pathological condition characterized by extreme anxiety about one's health

a ethnocentrism
b hypochondria
c nihilism
d catharsis
e hermaphroditism
f ontology
g aprosexia
h idiot savant
i psychasthenia
j megalomania

__________ **Score**
(5 points each)

Test 76

Not the Stars—Broadway Musicals

In this test you are asked to identify very popular musicals from Broadway from lists of performers who were "not the stars" but whose roles and performances were indispensable to the success of the shows.

The B.A. Level

_____ **1** Edith Adams; Stubby Kaye; Julie Newmar
_____ **2** Irving Jacobson; Joan Diener; Roy Middleton
_____ **3** Robert Goulet; Robert Coote; Roddy McDowall
_____ **4** Barbara Cook; David Burns; Eddie Hodges
_____ **5** Stanley Holloway; Robert Coote; Cathleen Nesbitt
_____ **6** William Tabbert; Juanita Hall; Myron McCormick
_____ **7** Maria Karnilova; Beatrice Arthur; Bert Convy
_____ **8** Rudy Vallee; Charles Nelson Reilly; Virginia Martin
_____ **9** Eddie Foy, Jr.; Carol Haney; Reta Shaw
_____ **10** Charles Winninger; Helen Morgan; Edna May Oliver

a *Camelot*
b *My Fair Lady*
c *How to Succeed in Business Without Really Trying*
d *Pajama Game*
e *Show Boat*
f *Li'l Abner*
g *South Pacific*
h *Man of La Mancha*
i *The Music Man*
j *Fiddler on the Roof*

_____ **Score**
(5 points each)

The M.S. Level

_____ **1** Jack Gilford; Bert Convy; Lotte Lenya
_____ **2** Chita Rivera; Susan Watson; Paul Lynde
_____ **3** Joan Diener; Richard Kiley; Henry Calvin
_____ **4** Larry Blyden; Keye Luke; Juanita Hall
_____ **5** Mimi Benzell; Molly Picon; Tommy Rall
_____ **6** Melba Moore; Shelley Plimpton; Diane Keaton
_____ **7** Jill O'Hara; Marian Mercer; Ken Howard
_____ **8** Theodore Bikel; Marion Marlowe; Kurt Kasznar
_____ **9** Sam Levene; Pat Rooney, Sr.; Stubby Kaye
_____ **10** Georgia Brown; David Jones; Bruce Prochnik

a *Kismet*
b *Promises, Promises*
c *Bye, Bye, Birdie*
d *Hair*
e *The Sound of Music*
f *Guys and Dolls*
g *Cabaret*
h *Oliver!*
i *Flower Drum Song*
j *Milk and Honey*

_____ **Score**
(5 points each)

The Ph.D. Level

_____ **1** Beatrice Arthur; Frankie Michaels; Jane Connell
_____ **2** David Burns; Jack Gilford; John Carradine
_____ **3** Walter Slezak; William Tabbert; Florence Henderson
_____ **4** Sydney Chaplin; Kay Medford; Danny Meehan
_____ **5** Daretta Morrow; Dorothy Sarnoff; Larry Douglas
_____ **6** David Burns; Eileen Brennan; Charles Nelson Reilly
_____ **7** Celeste Holm; Bambi Linn; Howard deSilva
_____ **8** Mickey Calin; Chita Rivera; Larry Kert
_____ **9** Richard Kiley; Noelle Adam; Alvin Epstein
_____ **10** Paula Wayne; Billy Daniels; Lola Falana

a *Fanny*
b *Funny Girl*
c *Golden Boy*
d *A Funny Thing Happened on the Way to the Forum*
e *West Side Story*
f *No Strings*
g *The King and I*
h *Hello, Dolly*
i *Oklahoma!*
j *Mame*

_____ **Score**
(5 points each)

Test 77

Hollywood Musicals—And the Songs Play On

Many songs which have become standards were featured in some of the great Hollywood musicals. Match the songs in this test with the musical in which it was introduced.

The B.A. Level

_____ **1** "Talk to the Animals"
_____ **2** "Swinging on a Star"
_____ **3** "True Love"
_____ **4** "Secret Love"
_____ **5** "Over the Rainbow"
_____ **6** "Wonderful Copenhagen"
_____ **7** "On the Atcheson, Topeka and the Santa Fe"
_____ **8** "Something's Gotta Give"
_____ **9** "Orchids in the Moonlight"
_____ **10** "You're Getting to Be a Habit With Me"

a *Calamity Jane*
b *High Society*
c *The Harvey Girls*
d *Going My Way*
e *Doctor Doolittle*
f *Daddy Long Legs*
g *The Wizard of Oz*
h *Flying Down to Rio*
i *Forty-Second Street*
j *Hans Christian Andersen*

________ **Score**
(5 points each)

The M.S. Level

_____ **1** "The Trolley Song"
_____ **2** "Sisters"
_____ **3** "Lonesome Polecat"
_____ **4** "I Fall in Love Too Easily"
_____ **5** "All by Myself"
_____ **6** "It Only Happens When I Dance with You"
_____ **7** "Ballin' the Jack"
_____ **8** "How Long Has This Been Going On"
_____ **9** "Thanks for the Memories"
_____ **10** "I'll Never Stop Loving You"

a *Anchors Aweigh*
b *The Big Broadcast of 1938*
c *Easter Parade*
d *For Me and My Girl*
e *Seven Brides for Seven Brothers*
f *Funny Face*
g *Blue Skies*
h *Love Me or Leave Me*
i *Meet Me in St. Louis*
j *White Christmas*

________ **Score**
(5 points each)

The Ph.D. Level

_____ **1** "Sometimes I'm Happy"
_____ **2** "Be Careful It's My Heart"
_____ **3** "It Had to Be You"
_____ **4** "A Spoonful of Sugar"
_____ **5** "They Can't Take That Away from Me"
_____ **6** "Stereophonic Sound"
_____ **7** "Accentuate the Positive"
_____ **8** "Busy Doing Nothing"
_____ **9** "How Could You Believe Me When I Said I Loved You?"
_____ **10** "Happiness Is Just a Thing Called Joe"

a *Cabin in the Sky*
b *Shall We Dance*
c *Hit the Deck*
d *Holiday Inn*
e *Here Comes the Waves*
f *A Connecticut Yankee at King Arthur's Court*
g *Mary Poppins*
h *I'll See You in My Dreams*
i *Royal Wedding*
j *Silk Stockings*

________ **Score**
(5 points each)

Test 78

The Name's the Same—A Reprise

Identify the pairs of "stars" from the following clues.

The B.A. Level

1.__________________ She starred with her husband, Rex Harrison, in *The Fourposter*. He was Li'l Abner.

2.__________________ He usually plays good ol' boys. She was the object of Gene Kelly's affection and was Jean Hagen's voice.

3.__________________ She won an Academy Award for being "friendly" to Montgomery Clift. He usually plays sullen leading men.

4.__________________ She was Kirk Douglas's wife in *Detective Story*. He was Davy Crockett.

5.__________________ He became famous during the Army-McCarthy hearings. She was a sex symbol of the late sixties.

6.__________________ She started as a child star, moved on to a brunette sex symbol. He starred with Greta Garbo in *Camille*.

7.__________________ He was Mr. Belevedere. He was Pete Kelly.

8.__________________ He removed a thorn from a lion's paw. She was the farmer's daughter.

9.__________________ She was an aquatic leading lady. He was Disney's *Zorro*.

10.__________________ She repeated her stage role as the evil child in *The Bad Seed*. He was Paul Newman's partner and manager.

__________**Score**
(5 points each)

The M.S. Level

1.__________________ He was Dagwood Bumstead. She was many times Alan Ladd's love interest.

2.__________________ His career took off when he broke with Jerry. Her film career was not as satisfactory as her stage appearances.

3.__________________ She is the widow of Ernie Kovacs. He was Will Stockdale's sidekick.

4.__________________ He was Jack Benny's valet. She was Mrs. Danvers in *Rebecca*.

5.__________________ He loved Laura. She didn't play her best stage role in the movies.

6.__________________ He was Natalie Wood's Jewish uncle. His son has been basically a character actor.

7.__________________ His biggest impact was as Chopin. He was the subject of two film biographies, one starring Robert Morley, the other Peter Finch.

8.__________________ He was Beauregard to Mame. She was a heavyweight "red hot mama."

9.__________________ He ruled that Edmund Gwenn was Santa Claus. She was Lassie's owner.

10.__________________ She was a child bride in her debut. He was Henry Tudor in *Richard III*.

__________**Score**
(5 points each)

Test 78

The Ph.D. Level

1.____________________ He was Mr. Waverly. She was the object of affection of both Gary Cooper and Preston Foster in *Canada*.

2.____________________ He often collaborated with Moss Hart. She was Tony Curtis's love in *Taras Bulba*.

3.____________________ She married Robert Wagner twice. He was the director of *For Whom the Bell Tolls*.

4.____________________ She was a teenage comedienne often teamed with Donald O'Connor. He was the major menace to Spencer Tracy at *Bad Rock*.

5.____________________ He was the director of *Anchors Aweigh*. She played the love of James Cagney in *Japan*.

__________**Score**
(5 points each)

6.____________________ She was portrayed by Kathryn Grayson in *So This Is Love*. He was a comedian with hesitant, bumbling manner.

7.____________________ She was adept at portraying not-so-dumb cheap blondes. He was a cabaret entertainer who is now a successful director.

8.____________________ Oscar Levant said he had seen every part of her except her forehead. He was Lt. Tragg.

9.____________________ She was typically a smooth socialite and one of the most beautiful women in Hollywood. His best role was Dillinger.

10.____________________ She played Cole Porter's wife in *Night and Day*. He played crusty, benevolent, or authoritarian old gentlemen.

Test 79

Major U.S. Corporations— Our Business Is Business

Our everyday purchases are the fuel of the nation's economy. In this test, you are asked to match leading U.S. corporations with their major products or services.

The B.A. Level

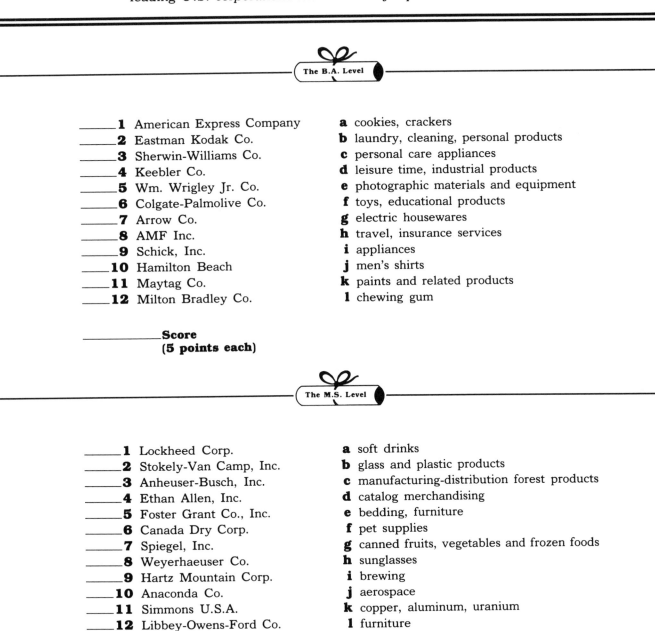

_____**1** American Express Company
_____**2** Eastman Kodak Co.
_____**3** Sherwin-Williams Co.
_____**4** Keebler Co.
_____**5** Wm. Wrigley Jr. Co.
_____**6** Colgate-Palmolive Co.
_____**7** Arrow Co.
_____**8** AMF Inc.
_____**9** Schick, Inc.
_____**10** Hamilton Beach
_____**11** Maytag Co.
_____**12** Milton Bradley Co.

a cookies, crackers
b laundry, cleaning, personal products
c personal care appliances
d leisure time, industrial products
e photographic materials and equipment
f toys, educational products
g electric housewares
h travel, insurance services
i appliances
j men's shirts
k paints and related products
l chewing gum

__________**Score**
(5 points each)

The M.S. Level

_____**1** Lockheed Corp.
_____**2** Stokely-Van Camp, Inc.
_____**3** Anheuser-Busch, Inc.
_____**4** Ethan Allen, Inc.
_____**5** Foster Grant Co., Inc.
_____**6** Canada Dry Corp.
_____**7** Spiegel, Inc.
_____**8** Weyerhaeuser Co.
_____**9** Hartz Mountain Corp.
_____**10** Anaconda Co.
_____**11** Simmons U.S.A.
_____**12** Libbey-Owens-Ford Co.

a soft drinks
b glass and plastic products
c manufacturing-distribution forest products
d catalog merchandising
e bedding, furniture
f pet supplies
g canned fruits, vegetables and frozen foods
h sunglasses
i brewing
j aerospace
k copper, aluminum, uranium
l furniture

__________**Score**
(5 points each)

Test 79

The Ph.D. Level

______1 The Trane Company	a wood and gypsum building products
______2 Heublein, Inc.	b labels
______3 Georgia-Pacific Corp.	c steam generating systems, air pollution control
______4 Fleetwood Enterprises, Inc.	d air conditioning, heat transfer equipment
______5 Avery International Corp.	e soft drink bottler, distribution
______6 Amstar Corp.	f mobile, motor homes, trailers
______7 A. E. Staley Manufacturing Co.	g opthalmic, scientific instruments
______8 MEI Corp.	h alcoholic beverages
______9 Gant Inc.	i sweeteners
______10 Babcock & Wilson Co.	j pharmaceuticals
______11 Merck & Co., Inc.	k corn and soybean processing
______12 Bausch & Lomb	l shirts, sportswear

__________**Score**
(5 points each)

Test **80**

Hail, Potpourri

The B.A. Level

1.____________________ What is the slogan of the Camp Fire Girls?

2.____________________ What is the name of the sailor boy on Cracker Jacks boxes?

3.____________________ At what college was the fraternity Phi Beta Kappa first organized?

4.____________________ What jockey rode Citation to the Triple Crown?

5.____________________ While on the island, Crichton was addressed as what?

6.____________________ What is the name of the Russian village in the musical play *Fiddler on the Roof*?

7.____________________ What was the only movie in which all the Barrymores, Lionel, Ethel and John appeared?

8.____________________ What is a pinochle?

9.____________________ What was the hometown of Mary Hartman?

10.____________________ Lord Jim became a wanderer in primitive places because . . .

__________**Score**
(5 points each)

The M.S. Level

1.____________________ An etymon is . . .

2.____________________ How does James Bond like his vodka martini made?

3.____________________ What trophy is awarded for the sport of badminton?

4.____________________ What was the name of the movie about Rocky Graziano?

5.____________________ *The Haunted Palace* by Frances Winwar is a biography of . . .

6.____________________ Who sang the song "I Made a Fool of Myself over John Foster Dulles"?

7.____________________ What was the name of the popular magazine which gave reading times for all articles?

8.____________________ What is the Peter Principle?

9.____________________ What race horse was named horse-of-the-year 1960 through 1964?

10.____________________ Mrs. Malaprop was called the queen of the . . .

__________**Score**
(5 points each)

The Ph.D. Level

1.____________________ What is a caesura?

2.____________________ What are halcyon days?

3.____________________ Who was the only Civil War soldier executed for war crimes?

4.____________________ What was the secret identity of Im-ho-Tep (the Mummy) played in the 1932 movie by Boris Karloff?

5.____________________ What is "a benign but mischievious creature. Very fond of rumpots, crackpots"?

6.____________________ What was the last line in the movie and novel *Gone with the Wind*?

7.____________________ Elinor Dashwood, Catherine Morland, and Anne Elliot are all characters from the work of . . .

8.____________________ Name the author and his work about the devil being outwitted by eloquence.

9.____________________ What do the letters stand for on J & B Rare Scotch bottles?

10.____________________ What are the four state capitals named after American Presidents?

__________**Score**
(5 points each)

Test
81

Military Men—Let the Battles Begin

One way to study history is through the military battles and their effect on the life of the world. The military leaders in this test should be easy to identify.

The B.A. Level

______**1** aided American cause in the revolution	**a** David Farragut
______**2** headed Third Army invasion of German-occupied Europe	**b** Horatio Nelson
______**3** Sioux war chief victorious at Little Big Horn	**c** George Dewey
______**4** naval commander, destroyed French fleet at Trafalgar	**d** Marquis de Lafayette
______**5** headed Green Mountain Boys	**e** Stephen Decatur
______**6** Union Admiral captured New Orleans, Mobile Bay	**f** George S. Patton
______**7** commanded *Bonhomme Richard* in victory over Serapis	**g** Ethan Allen
______**8** naval hero of Barbary wars	**h** Benedict Arnold
______**9** victorious at Saratoga, tried to betray West Point to Britain	**i** Crazy Horse
______**10** destroyed Spanish fleet at Manila	**j** John Paul Jones

__________**Score**
(5 points each)

The M.S. Level

______**1** commander of naval forces in Pacific in W.W. II	**a** Henry "Hap" Arnold
______**2** sacked Atlanta during "march to sea"	**b** Oliver Perry
______**3** commanded Army Air Force in W.W. II	**c** Pierre Beauregard
______**4** organized revolt of Arabs against Turks	**d** Charles G. Gordon
______**5** won battle of Lake Erie in War of 1812	**e** William T. Sherman
______**6** led forces in China, killed at Khartoum	**f** Erwin Rommel
______**7** Confederate general, ordered bombardment of Ft. Sumter	**g** John Burgoyne
______**8** defeated Japanese fleet at Leyte Gulf	**h** Thomas E. Lawrence
______**9** headed Afrika Korps in W.W. II	**i** Chester Nimitz
______**10** defeated at Saratoga	**j** William F. Halsey

__________**Score**
(5 points each)

The Ph.D. Level

______**1** commanded forces in Vietnam, 1968–72	**a** George Meade
______**2** commanded Union forces at Gettysburg	**b** Creighton Abrams
______**3** led charge at Gettysburg	**c** Lucius D. Clay
______**4** defeated Indians at Fallen Timbers	**d** George B. McClellan
______**5** led Berlin airlift	**e** Horatio H. Kitchener
______**6** won battle of the Marne	**f** Jonathan M. Wainwright
______**7** forced to surrender on Corregidor	**g** Joseph Joffre
______**8** headed forces in Mexican War	**h** George E. Pickett
______**9** led forces in Boer War	**i** Anthony Wayne
______**10** Union general commanded Army of the Potomac	**j** Winfield Scott

__________**Score**
(5 points each)

Test 82

Authors and Their Works—A Reprise

Identify two works of the given authors and playwrights.

The B.A. Level

____ **1** George Bernard Shaw	**a** *The Adventures of Augie March*	**k** *Androcles and the Lion*
____ **2** J. D. Salinger	**b** *A Clockwork Orange*	**l** *The Power and the Glory*
____ **3** Vladimir Nabokov	**c** *Portnoy's Complaint*	**m** *The Second Sex*
____ **4** Anthony Burgess	**d** *A Very Easy Death*	**n** *The Catcher in the Rye*
____ **5** Graham Greene	**e** *The Man With the Golden Arm*	**o** *One Hand Clapping*
____ **6** Simone de Beauvoir	**f** *Major Barbara*	**p** *Herzog*
____ **7** Nelson Algren	**g** *Pale Fire*	**q** *Go Tell It on the Mountain*
____ **8** Philip Roth	**h** *Goodbye Columbus*	**r** *Lolita*
____ **9** James Baldwin	**i** *Franny and Zooey*	**s** *The Fire Next Time*
____ **10** Saul Bellow	**j** *A Walk on the Wild Side*	**t** *The Heart of the Matter*

________ **Score**
(5 points each)

The M.S. Level

____ **1** Pearl Buck	**a** *The Group*	**k** *The Homecoming*
____ **2** Irwin Shaw	**b** *Fear of Flying*	**l** *The Humanist in the Bathtub*
____ **3** Herman Wouk	**c** *Tortilla Flat*	**m** *Two Weeks in Another Town*
____ **4** Mary McCarthy	**d** *Love Is Eternal*	**n** *O Pioneers!*
____ **5** Harold Pinter	**e** *Dragon Seed*	**o** *The Fires of Spring*
____ **6** Erica Jong	**f** *The Young Lions*	**p** *Aurora Dawn*
____ **7** Willa Cather	**g** *The Agony and the Ecstasy*	**q** *The Caretaker*
____ **8** James Michener	**h** *Satan Never Sleeps*	**r** *The Scource*
____ **9** John Steinbeck	**i** *Fanny*	**s** *Marjorie Morningstar*
____ **10** Irving Stone	**j** *My Antonia*	**t** *Cannery Row*

________ **Score**
(5 points each)

The Ph.D. Level

____ **1** Flannery O'Connor	**a** *The Zoo Story*	**k** *Final Payments*
____ **2** Mary Gordon	**b** *Erewhon*	**l** *By Love Possessed*
____ **3** Agatha Christie	**c** *The Wapshot Chronicle*	**m** *The Company of Women*
____ **4** Edward Albee	**d** *The Way of All Flesh*	**n** *A Song of Sixpence*
____ **5** A. J. Cronin	**e** *Wise Blood*	**o** *Giles Goat Boy*
____ **6** John Cheever	**f** *Murder in Three Acts*	**p** *The Sot-Weed Factor*
____ **7** William Burroughs	**g** *The Violent Bear It Away*	**q** *Nova Express*
____ **8** John Barth	**h** *Naked Lunch*	**r** *Hatter's Castle*
____ **9** James Cozzens	**i** *Tiny Alice*	**s** *Bullet Park*
____ **10** Samuel Butler	**j** *The Mousetrap*	**t** *The Just and the Unjust*

________ **Score**
(5 points each)

Test
83

Song Titles—Old Favorites

Match the following songs with their first lines.

The B.A. Level

_____**1** "The stars at night are big and bright . . ."
_____**2** "I wish I was in the land of cotton . . ."
_____**3** "Dashing through the snow . . ."
_____**4** "O say! can you see . . ."
_____**5** "My country 'tis of thee . . ."
_____**6** "O beautiful, for spacious skies . . ."
_____**7** "O bury me not . . ."
_____**8** "I come from Alabama . . ."
_____**9** "Way down upon de Swannee River . . ."
_____**10** "Lullaby and good night . . ."

a "Jingle Bells"
b "America"
c "The Lone Prairie"
d "Cradle Song"
e "Oh! Susanna"
f "Deep in the Heart of Texas"
g "Old Folks at Home"
h "The Star-Spangled Banner"
i "America, the Beautiful"
j "Dixie"

__________**Score**
(5 points each)

The M.S. Level

_____**1** "When you hear that the preaching does begin . . ."
_____**2** "You got a gal and I got none . . ."
_____**3** "Look down, look down . . ."
_____**4** "Oh, give me a home where the buffalo roam . . ."
_____**5** "Skeeters are a hummin' on de honey suckle vine . . ."
_____**6** "I've got a mule, her name is Sal . . ."
_____**7** "So get out of the way . . ."
_____**8** "Jes' a lookin' for a home . . ."
_____**9** "Every little breeze seems to whisper . . ."
_____**10** "Jimmy crack corn an' ah don' care . . ."

a "Home on the Range"
b "Old Dan Tucker"
c "Kentucky Babe"
d "Louise"
e "The Boll Weevil "
f "Li'l Liza Jane"
g "De Blue Tail Fly"
h "The Erie Canal"
i "There'll Be a Hot Time in the Old Town Tonight"
j "Lonesome Road"

__________**Score**
(5 points each)

The Ph.D. Level

_____**1** "I've been workin' on de railroad . . ."
_____**2** "There's a garden, what a garden . . ."
_____**3** "Goin' to run all night . . ."
_____**4** "Whoopee ti yi yo . . ."
_____**5** "Casey would waltz with a strawberry blonde . . ."
_____**6** "Put on de skillet, put on de led . . ."
_____**7** "Day is done . . ."
_____**8** "Daisy, Daisy, give me your answer true . . ."
_____**9** "Keep a-movin', Dan . . ."
_____**10** "My daddy is an engineer . . ."

a "Beer Barrel Polka"
b "The Band Played On"
c "A Bicycle Built for Two"
d "Cool Water"
e "Taps"
f "Levee Song"
g "Camptown Races"
h "Git Along Little Dogies"
i "Wanderin'"
j "Shortnin' Bread"

__________**Score**
(5 points each)

Test 84

Science Fiction Movies—Come into My Laboratory

Not all science fiction buffs are trivia fans, but all trivia fans are science fiction buffs—or is it the other way around? Oh well, why worry unless some creature, some robot, some monster is tracking you. As a mathematician, I always resented the fact that the only mathematicians who ever appeared in movies were beautiful Ph. D.s who didn't have enough sense to stay out of the clutches of some sinister force. Never mind; just match the science fiction movies with the director, and may the force be with you.

The B.A. Level

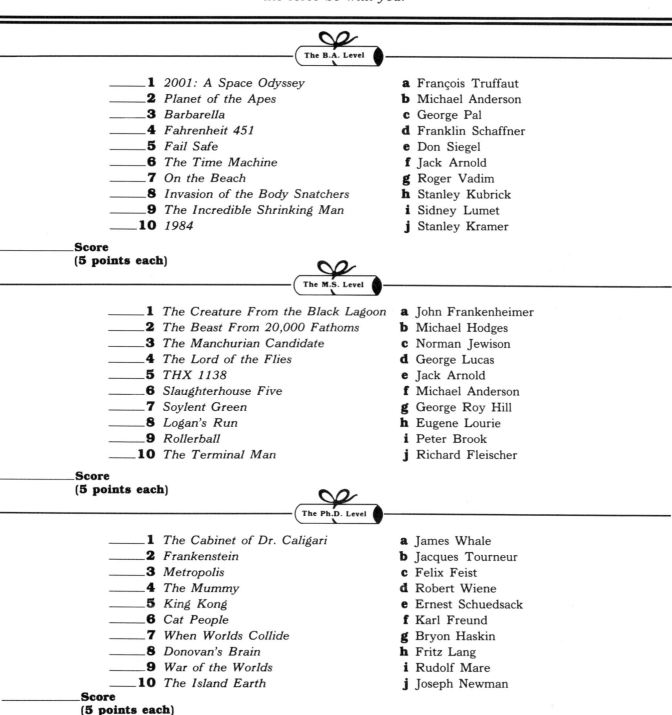

____ **1** *2001: A Space Odyssey*	**a** François Truffaut
____ **2** *Planet of the Apes*	**b** Michael Anderson
____ **3** *Barbarella*	**c** George Pal
____ **4** *Fahrenheit 451*	**d** Franklin Schaffner
____ **5** *Fail Safe*	**e** Don Siegel
____ **6** *The Time Machine*	**f** Jack Arnold
____ **7** *On the Beach*	**g** Roger Vadim
____ **8** *Invasion of the Body Snatchers*	**h** Stanley Kubrick
____ **9** *The Incredible Shrinking Man*	**i** Sidney Lumet
____ **10** *1984*	**j** Stanley Kramer

________ **Score**
(5 points each)

The M.S. Level

____ **1** *The Creature From the Black Lagoon*	**a** John Frankenheimer
____ **2** *The Beast From 20,000 Fathoms*	**b** Michael Hodges
____ **3** *The Manchurian Candidate*	**c** Norman Jewison
____ **4** *The Lord of the Flies*	**d** George Lucas
____ **5** *THX 1138*	**e** Jack Arnold
____ **6** *Slaughterhouse Five*	**f** Michael Anderson
____ **7** *Soylent Green*	**g** George Roy Hill
____ **8** *Logan's Run*	**h** Eugene Lourie
____ **9** *Rollerball*	**i** Peter Brook
____ **10** *The Terminal Man*	**j** Richard Fleischer

________ **Score**
(5 points each)

The Ph.D. Level

____ **1** *The Cabinet of Dr. Caligari*	**a** James Whale
____ **2** *Frankenstein*	**b** Jacques Tourneur
____ **3** *Metropolis*	**c** Felix Feist
____ **4** *The Mummy*	**d** Robert Wiene
____ **5** *King Kong*	**e** Ernest Schuedsack
____ **6** *Cat People*	**f** Karl Freund
____ **7** *When Worlds Collide*	**g** Bryon Haskin
____ **8** *Donovan's Brain*	**h** Fritz Lang
____ **9** *War of the Worlds*	**i** Rudolf Mare
____ **10** *The Island Earth*	**j** Joseph Newman

________ **Score**
(5 points each)

Test 85

Who Was That?—The Fabulous Fifties' Movies

Midlife, so far, for the author, was the fifties—still an age of innocence, but the future could be seen on the horizon—the turmoil of the sixties, the destruction of the seventies, and the what of the eighties. Return with me to those simpler days and identify the actors who played the characters in some memorable movies.

The B.A. Level

___	**1** Addison DeWitt	**a**	Ernest Borgnine	**I**	*The Quiet Man*
___	**2** Angelo Maggio	**b**	Lee J. Cobb	**II**	*A Streetcar Named Desire*
___	**3** Marty Pilletti	**c**	Marilyn Monroe	**III**	*All About Eve*
___	**4** Johnny Friendly	**d**	Marlon Brando	**IV**	*Around the World in 80 Days*
___	**5** Sean Thornton	**e**	Cary Grant	**V**	*On the Waterfront*
___	**6** Joey Starrett	**f**	George Sanders	**VI**	*From Here to Eternity*
___	**7** Stanley Kowalski	**g**	David Niven	**VII**	*Some Like It Hot*
___	**8** John Robie	**h**	John Wayne	**VIII**	*Marty*
___	**9** Phineas Fogg	**i**	Brandon de Wilde	**IX**	*To Catch a Thief*
___	**10** Sugar Kane	**j**	Frank Sinatra	**X**	*Shane*

______ **Score**
(5 points each)

The M.S. Level

___	**1** Esther Blodgett	**a**	James Mason	**I**	*The Bridge on the River Kwai*
___	**2** Norma Desmond	**b**	Lana Turner	**II**	*Five Fingers*
___	**3** Mike Ribble	**c**	Alec Guinness	**III**	*A Star is Born*
___	**4** Cicero	**d**	Glenn Ford	**IV**	*Singin' in the Rain*
___	**5** James McLeod	**e**	Judy Garland	**V**	*Trapeze*
___	**6** Colonel Nicholson	**f**	Grace Kelly	**VI**	*Sunset Boulevard*
___	**7** Richard Dadier	**g**	Burt Lancaster	**VII**	*Peyton Place*
___	**8** Amy Kane	**h**	Gene Kelly	**VIII**	*Detective Story*
___	**9** Don Lockwood	**i**	Kirk Douglas	**IX**	*High Noon*
___	**10** Constance McKenzie	**j**	Gloria Swanson	**X**	*The Blackboard Jungle*

______ **Score**
(5 points each)

The Ph.D. Level

___	**1** Wilson	**a**	Spencer Tracy	**I**	*A Place in the Sun*
___	**2** Madge Owens	**b**	Tom Ewell	**II**	*Born Yesterday*
___	**3** J. J. Hunsecker	**c**	Kim Novak	**III**	*Bad Day at Black Rock*
___	**4** John T. Macready	**d**	Sam Jaffe	**IV**	*Shane*
___	**5** Harry Powell	**e**	Jack Palance	**V**	*Picnic*
___	**6** Richard Sherman	**f**	Doris Day	**VI**	*The Seven-Year Itch*
___	**7** Alice Tripp	**g**	Judy Holliday	**VII**	*The Asphalt Jungle*
___	**8** Jan Morrow	**h**	Burt Lancaster	**VIII**	*The Night of the Hunter*
___	**9** Billie Dawn	**i**	Shelley Winters	**IX**	*Pillow Talk*
___	**10** Erwin Riedenschneider	**j**	Robert Mitchum	**X**	*Sweet Smell of Success*

______ **Score**
(5 points each)

Test
86

Artists—Sculptures—I Created a Masterpiece

Here we are in Art Appreciation 100. All right, students, show your culture by matching the artists with their works.

The B.A. Level

_____ **1** *The Persistence of Memory*
_____ **2** *At the Moulin Rouge*
_____ **3** *David*
_____ **4** *The Birth of Venus*
_____ **5** *Mona Lisa*
_____ **6** *Ballet Rehearsal*
_____ **7** *The Gleaners*
_____ **8** *Liberty Leading the People*
_____ **9** *The Scream*
_____ **10** *Portrait of Gertrude Stein*

a Edgar Degas
b Sandro Botticelli
c Pablo Picasso
d Edvard Munch
e Salvador Dali
f Michelangelo
g Eugene Delacroix
h Henri de Toulouse-Lautrec
i Jean Francois Millet
j Leonardo da Vinci

__________ **Score**
(5 points each)

The M.S. Level

_____ **1** *Christina's World*
_____ **2** *Soft Toilet*
_____ **3** *The Death of Marat*
_____ **4** *The Spirit of the Dead Watching*
_____ **5** *Lucifer*
_____ **6** *Bird in Space*
_____ **7** *The Night Cafe*
_____ **8** *Death and Fire*
_____ **9** *Reclining Figure*
_____ **10** *Giovanni Arnolfini and His Bride*

a Jan van Eyck
b Henry Moore
c Jackson Pollock
d Vincent van Gogh
e Jacques Louis David
f Paul Klee
g Claes Oldenburg
h Constantin Brancusi
i Andrew Wyeth
j Paul Gauguin

__________ **Score**
(5 points each)

The Ph.D. Level

_____ **1** *Young Woman with a Water Jug*
_____ **2** *The Third of May*
_____ **3** *The Swing*
_____ **4** *Syndier of the Cloth Guild*
_____ **5** *The Martyrdom of St. Sebastian*
_____ **6** *Melancolia I*
_____ **7** *Red Room*
_____ **8** *Composition in Blue, Yellow, and Black*
_____ **9** *The Third Class Carriage*
_____ **10** *Grand Odalisque*

a Jean-Honoré Fragonard
b Honoré Daumier
c Antonello da Messina
d Jan Vermeer
e Piet Mondrian
f Francisco Goya
g Henri Matisse
h Rembrandt van Rijn
i Jean-Auguste-Dominique Ingres
j Albrecht Dürer

__________ **Score**
(5 points each)

Test
87

Sports Quotes—You Know Me, Al

Jocks are not usually known for their wisdom, and the quotes chosen here do not necessarily refute the thought, but they are often at least amusing and insightful. Match the quote with the quoter.

The B.A. Level

_____**1** "I am the greatest"
_____**2** "Don't look back. Something might be gaining on you."
_____**3** "It's a great day for a game. Let's play two."
_____**4** "Is Brooklyn still in the league?"
_____**5** "The future is now."
_____**6** "Winning isn't everything, but it beats anything that comes in second."
_____**7** "Nice guys finish last."
_____**8** "Winning isn't everything; it's the only thing."
_____**9** "A tie is like kissing your sister."
_____**10** "Hit 'em where they ain't."

a Wee Willie Keeler
b Billy Terry
c Vince Lombardi
d Bear Bryant
e Duffy Daughtery
f Muhammad Ali
g Leo Durocher
h Ernie Banks
i Leroy "Satchel" Paige
j George Allen

__________**Score**
(5 points each)

The M.S. Level

_____**1** ". . . today I count myself the luckiest of men on the face of the earth."
_____**2** "With the money I'm making, I should be playing two positions."
_____**3** "Ya gotta believe."
_____**4** "The opera's not over until the fat lady sings."
_____**5** "If I was playing in New York, they'd name a candy bar after me."
_____**6** "I never was hurt by a punch I saw."
_____**7** "You could look it up."
_____**8** "Float like a butterfly; sting like a bee."
_____**9** "You gotta be a man to play baseball for a living, but you gotta have a lot of little boy in you, too."
_____**10** "I fought Sugar Ray Robinson so many times it's a wonder I didn't get diabetes."

a Jake LaMotta
b Reggie Jackson
c Bundini Brown
d Pete Rose
e Casey Stengel
f Lou Gehrig
g Roy Campanella
h Dick Motta
i Tug McGraw
j Gene Fulmer

__________**Score**
(5 points each)

Test 87

The Ph.D. Level

_____ **1** "All pro athletes are bilingual. They speak English and profanity."
_____ **2** "Gentlemen, you are about to play football for Yale. Never again in your life will you do anything so important."
_____ **3** "All I ever wanted to be president of was the American League."
_____ **4** "Shut up! He explained."
_____ **5** "I went to a fight the other night and a hockey game broke out."
_____ **6** "If I knew what horse would win, I wouldn't be riding, I'd be betting."
_____ **7** "Close don't count in baseball, close only counts in horseshoes and grenades."
_____ **8** "If there is any larceny in a man, golf will bring it out."
_____ **9** "When you're a pro, you come back no matter what happened the day before."
_____ **10** "I want my teams to have my personality—surly, obnoxious, and arrogant."

a Rodney Dangerfield
b Ring Lardner
c Gordie Howe
d Al McGuire
e Paul Gallico
f Tad Jones
g Billy Martin
h A. Bartlett Giamatti
i Don Brumfield
j Frank Robinson

_____ **Score**
(5 points each)

Test 88

The Simple Statement of the Plot—Movies

Each of the movies identified in this test by a brief plot line has won at least one Academy Award for acting, directing, producing, song, or story. Name them.

The B.A. Level

1.____________________ a young teenager is obsessed with an attractive war bride during one lazy idyllic summer

2.____________________ a former cat burglar is forced out of retirement by a new thief who is copying his methods

3.____________________ the desperate infighting between a professor and his shrewish wife and an innocent young faculty couple

4.____________________ a former dancer and her daughter are forced to share their Manhattan apartment with an aspiring young actor

5.____________________ a young lawyer-civil rights worker is turned into a Kennedy style U.S. Senator by his party's machine politicians

6.____________________ an American writer tries to persuade a happy-go-lucky prostitute to concentrate on the high-minded ideals of Aristotle

7.____________________ a thick-witted small town police chief is forced to investigate a murder with the help of a black homicide expert from Philadelphia

8.____________________ a private eye searching for a missing suburban husband works with a call girl who numbered the husband among her clients

9.____________________ a well-educated young lady turns outlaw to avenge her father's death

10.____________________ a wandering young hobo arrives in a small town on Labor Day and changes the lives of several of the inhabitants

11.____________________ an infamous racketeer in watered-down penicillin is tracked down in postwar Vienna

12.____________________ the funny and sad experiences of an elderly widower traveling across America with his cat

__________**Score**
(5 points each)

The M.S. Level

1.____________________ a plain spinster is wooed for her money by a handsome fortune hunter

2.____________________ a bittersweet love story about a feckless would-be actress and a blind young songwriter

3.____________________ a deaf-mute farm girl is befriended and educated by a kindly local doctor after being raped by a drunken seaman

4.____________________ a romantic and excitable young girl marries the simple, plodding schoolteacher and has an affair with a shell-shocked young British officer

5.____________________ a failed novelist is driven to the verge of suicide by his addiction to drink

6.____________________ a drunken demented ex-child star gets her kicks by slowly torturing her crippled sister

7.____________________ the childhood of a young girl and her relationships with her friends, neighbors, and parents as she grows up in a tenement in the 1900s

8.____________________ the individual personal dramas of a group of guests at a British seaside resort hotel

9.____________________ an unemployed actress with ten shares in a vast corporation proceeds to prove that the board of directors is riddled with corruption

10.____________________ a widow with a teenage son tries to make an independent life for herself but learns just how difficult it can be

11.____________________ a struggling artist becomes infatuated with a young woman who turns out to be no more than the spirit of a girl who died several years before

12.____________________ the story of farming peasants fighting for survival in prerevolutionary China

__________**Score**
(5 points each)

Test 88

The Ph.D. Level

1.____________________ the stormy marriage of '20s torch singer Ruth Etting and a tough racketeer

2.____________________ an idealistic young man sheds his rich background to search for faith and spiritual fulfillment in his life

3.____________________ a girl from the wrong side of the tracks falls in love with a handsome socialite but eventually finds happiness with a man from her own level of society

4.____________________ earthy flamenco dancer becomes a major Hollywood star and then rejects the tinsel world she has conquered

5.____________________ a runaway heiress and a journalist form a lasting relationship in their journey across country

6.____________________ a well-heeled married insurance agent drifts into an innocent affair with a smart young woman and finds himself over-involved romantically

7.____________________ the emotional and business problems of a smalltime promoter-widower who operates a fleabag hotel in Miami Beach

8.____________________ a chauffeur's daughter is romanced by the two sons of a wealthy Long Island family

9.____________________ an amnesiac doctor who subconsciously believes himself to be a murderer is helped by a woman psychiatrist to prove his innocence

10.____________________ a medical health officer and a weary cop track down an on-the-run criminal carrying a deadly plague germ

11.____________________ a Sicilian-born peasant mourns deeply for her dead truck driver husband and settles for a great sweating oaf of a man

12.____________________ a wealthy young wife believes that her irresponsible playboy husband is trying to murder her

____________**Score**
(5 points each)

Test 89

The Big Bands—Theme Songs

All right, folks, let's dance. Match the band leader with his theme song.

The B.A. Level

____ **1** "Does Your Heart Beat for Me?"	**a** Ray Anthony
____ **2** "Scatterbrain"	**b** Orrin Tucker
____ **3** "The Man with a Horn"	**c** Jimmy Dorsey
____ **4** "Contrasts"	**d** Les Brown
____ **5** "Drifting and Dreaming"	**e** Jackie Gleason
____ **6** "Star Burst"	**f** Russ Morgan
____ **7** "Babalu"	**g** Fletcher Henderson
____ **8** "Melancholy Serenade"	**h** Gene Krupa
____ **9** "Sentimental Journey"	**i** Frankie Masters
____ **10** "Christopher Columbus"	**j** Desi Arnaz

________ **Score**
(5 points each)

The M.S. Level

____ **1** "Howdy, Friends"	**a** Red Nichols
____ **2** "I May Be Wrong"	**b** Bob Crosby
____ **3** "Hot Lips"	**c** Ray McKinley
____ **4** "Singing Winds"	**d** Tony Pastor
____ **5** "Wailing to the Four Winds"	**e** Chick Webb
____ **6** "Blossoms"	**f** Xavier Cugat
____ **7** "My Shawl"	**g** Henry Busse
____ **8** "You Go to My Head"	**h** Billy May
____ **9** "Lean Baby"	**i** Ralph Flanagan
____ **10** "Summertime"	**j** Mitchell Ayres

________ **Score**
(5 points each)

The Ph.D. Level

____ **1** "I Would Do Anything for You"	**a** Claude Thornhill
____ **2** "Snowfall"	**b** Will Bradley
____ **3** "Sunset to Sunrise"	**c** Raymond Scott
____ **4** "Celery Stalks at Midnight"	**d** Hal Kemp
____ **5** "Day Dreams Come True at Night"	**e** Claude Hopkins
____ **6** "Pretty Little Petticoat"	**f** Art Mooney
____ **7** "Dipsy Doodle"	**g** Dirk Jurgens
____ **8** "Sometimes I'm Happy"	**h** Jimmy Lunceford
____ **9** "How I Miss You When Summer Is Gone"	**i** Blue Barron
____ **10** "Jazznocracy"	**j** Larry Clinton

________ **Score**
(5 points each)

Test 90

Carry Me Back to Old Potpourri

The B.A. Level

1.____________________ What was the name of the female plumber in TV Comet cleanser commercials played by Jane Withers?

2.____________________ What is the low man (woman) in marks in West Point graduation classes called?

3.____________________ What Shakespeare play contains the line "What's in a name?"

4.____________________ How did Mark Antony commit suicide?

5.____________________ Who sponsored Jack Armstrong on radio?

6.____________________ What was the 48th State admitted to the Union?

7.____________________ What was the real name of Lewis Carroll?

8.____________________ What was the name of Dorothy's aunt in *The Wizard of Oz*?

9.____________________ What city is the location of all the streets mentioned in the game of Monopoly?

10.____________________ What drink does Dennis the Menace recommend with cookies?

__________**Score**
(5 points each)

The M.S. Level

1.____________________ Who was the dwarf who could spin straw into gold?

2.____________________ Who is the patron saint of England?

3.____________________ Who is Dick Tracy's freckle-faced detective companion?

4.____________________ What is the Scout slogan?

5.____________________ What is the name of the third child of Adam and Eve?

6.____________________ What was the name of Vaughn Monroe's four-member female backup vocal group?

7.____________________ What was the desert mountain where Moses received the Ten Commandments?

8.____________________ What was the name of King Arthur's sword?

9.____________________ Who is the New York photographer who hounded Jacqueline Kennedy Onassis for a number of years?

10.____________________ The lines "Home is the place where, when you have to go there, they have to take you in" were written by . . .

__________**Score**
(5 points each)

The Ph.D. Level

1.____________________ In what modern novel would you find Daisy and Tom Buchanan?

2.____________________ Name the *Alexandria Quartet* by Lawrence Durrell.

3.____________________ Who wrote the lines "This is the way the world ends. Not with a bang but a whimper"?

4.____________________ What was the name of Benito Mussolini's mistress who was executed with him?

5.____________________ What was the green-covered magazine founded and edited by H. L. Mencken and George Jean Nathan?

6.____________________ What product was advertised by the slogan "Ask the man who owns one"?

7.____________________ Who was known as the Lady of Bedloes Island?

8.____________________ In what city would the Hotel Raffles be found?

9.____________________ What is a palindrome?

10.____________________ In what city will you find Antoine's?

__________**Score**
(5 points each)

Test
91

And Then I Directed—A Reprise

Select the movie that was not *the work of the given director.*

The B.A. Level

_______**1** Norman Jewison: **a.** *The Cincinnati Kid* **b.** *The Kremlin Letter* **c.** *In the Heat of the Night* **d.** *Fiddler on the Roof*

_______**2** Stanley Kubrick: **a.** *Under Capricorn* **b.** *Paths of Glory* **c.** *Lolita* **d.** *Dr. Strangelove*

_______**3** Joshua Logan: **a.** *Camelot* **b.** *South Pacific* **c.** *Bus Stop* **d.** *Kismet*

_______**4** Paul Newman: **a.** *Rachel, Rachel* **b.** *W.U.S.A.* **c.** *The Effect of Gamma Rays on Man-in-the-Moon Marigolds* **d.** *Sometimes a Great Notion*

_______**5** Tony Richardson: **a.** *Oh Dad, Poor Dad* **b.** *A Taste of Honey* **c.** *Tom Jones* **d.** *The Loneliness of the Long Distance Runner*

_______**6** George Stevens: **a.** *A Place in the Sun* **b.** *Giant* **c.** *The Hairy Ape* **d.** *The Diary of Anne Frank*

_______**7** Raoul Walsh: **a.** *High Sierra* **b.** *White Heat* **c.** *Little Caesar* **d.** *The Bowery*

_______**8** William Wyler: **a.** *Mrs. Miniver* **b.** *The Best Years of Our Lives* **c.** *Ben Hur* **d.** *Our Town*

_______**9** Fred Zinnemann: **a.** *The Men* **b.** *High Noon* **c.** *Murder, Inc.* **d.** *The Nun's Story*

_______**10** Ingmar Bergman: **a.** *Cries and Whispers* **b.** *Electra* **c.** *Smiles of a Summer Night* **d.** *Persona*

__________**Score**
(5 points each)

The M.S. Level

_______**1** Francis Ford Coppola: **a.** *Five Easy Pieces* **b.** *Finian's Rainbow* **c.** *Apocalypse Now* **d.** *The Conversation*

_______**2** Stanley Donen: **a.** *Damn Yankees* **b.** *Charade* **c.** *The Pajama Game* **d.** *The Ipcress File*

_______**3** Federico Fellini: **a.** *La Dolce Vita* **b.** *The Garden of the Finzi-Continis* **c.** *8½* **d.** *La Strada*

_______**4** Victor Fleming: **a.** *Treasure Island* **b.** *Brute Force* **c.** *The Wizard of Oz* **d.** *Tortilla Flat*

_______**5** Michelangelo Antonioni: **a.** *Umberto D* **b.** *L'Avventura* **c.** *The Red Desert* **d.** *Zabriskie Point*

_______**6** William Dietele: **a.** *San Quentin* **b.** *The Hunchback of Notre Dame* **c.** *Portrait of Jennie* **d.** *Juarez*

_______**7** Sam Wood: **a.** *For Whom the Bell Tolls* **b.** *The Devil and Miss Jones* **c.** *Wuthering Heights* **d.** *Goodbye Mr. Chips*

_______**8** Frank Perry: **a.** *Diary of a Mad Housewife* **b.** *The Long Hot Summer* **c.** *The Swimmer* **d.** *David and Lisa*

_______**9** Nicholas Ray: **a.** *Peyton Place* **b.** *Rebel Without a Cause* **c.** *55 Days at Peking* **d.** *In a Lonely Place*

_______**10** Carol Reed: **a.** *Oliver!* **b.** *Our Man in Havana* **c.** *The Key* **d.** *The Best Man*

__________**Score**
(5 points each)

Test 91

The Ph.D. Level

_____**1** Franklin Schaffner: **a.** *Papillon* **b.** *Patton* **c.** *The War Lord* **d.** *Von Ryan's Express*

_____**2** Richard Quine: **a.** *The Solid Gold Cadillac* **b.** *The Jolson Story* **c.** *The World of Suzie Wong* **d.** *Bell, Book and Candle*

_____**3** Walter Lang: **a.** *Green Pastures* **b.** *State Fair* **c.** *The King and I* **d.** *Call Me Madam*

_____**4** Martin Ritt: **a.** *Hud* **b.** *The Long Hot Summer* **c.** *Cool Hand Luke* **d.** *The Spy Who Came in From the Cold*

_____**5** Vincent Sherman: **a.** *All Through the Night* **b.** *This Gun for Hire* **c.** *Mr. Skeffington* **d.** *Old Acquaintance*

_____**6** George Seaton: **a.** *The Hustler* **b.** *Miracle on 34th Street* **c.** *The Country Girl* **d.** *The Counterfeit Traitor*

_____**7** William Wellman: **a.** *The High and the Mighty* **b.** *Blood Alley* **c.** *Track of the Cat* **d.** *The Tarnished Angels*

_____**8** Preston Sturges: **a.** *Sullivan's Travels* **b.** *The Miracle of Morgan's Creek* **c.** *Hail the Conquering Hero* **d.** *The Farmer's Daughter*

_____**9** Luchino Visconti: **a.** *The Butcher* **b.** *The Leopard* **c.** *The Damned* **d.** *Rocco and His Brothers*

_____**10** Charles Walters: **a.** *Don't Go Near the Water* **b.** *The Teahouse of the August Moon* **c.** *Please Don't Eat the Daisies* **d.** *The Unsinkable Molly Brown*

_____**Score**
(5 points each)

Test 92

Still More Double Features

Match the actors and actresses with a pair of their films.

The B.A. Level

_____ 1 *Mrs. Miniver* and *The Bad and The Beautiful*
_____ 2 *Isadora* and *Camelot*
_____ 3 *Come Blow Your Horn* and *Pal Joey*
_____ 4 *The French Line* and *The Revolt of Mamie Stover*
_____ 5 *Dial M for Murder* and *Love Story*
_____ 6 *Taras Bulba* and *Fuzz*
_____ 7 *Million Dollar Mermaid* and *Neptune's Daughter*
_____ 8 *Serpico* and *The Godfather*
_____ 9 *Viva Maria* and *The Devil is a Woman*
_____ 10 *Harper* and *Blood Alley*
_____ 11 *Kitty Foyle* and *Black Widow*
_____ 12 *Murder My Sweet* and *Susan Slept Here*

a Jane Russell
b Dick Powell
c Ray Milland
d Walter Pidgeon
e Esther Williams
f Lauren Bacall
g Brigitte Bardot
h Vanessa Redgrave
i Frank Sinatra
j Ginger Rogers
k Yul Brynner
l Al Pacino

_____ **Score**
(5 points each)

The M.S. Level

_____ 1 *Jeremiah Johnson* and *The Great Gatsby*
_____ 2 *Jesse James* and *The Razor's Edge*
_____ 3 *The Counterfeit Traitor* and *The Fourposter*
_____ 4 *Foreign Correspondent* and *Buffalo Bill*
_____ 5 *The Damned* and *The Doctor's Dilemma*
_____ 6 *Father of the Bride* and *The Macomber Affair*
_____ 7 *The Dark at the Top of the Stairs* and *Our Miss Brooks*
_____ 8 *Roman Holiday* and *Oklahoma!*
_____ 9 *Night of the Hunter* and *The Last Time I Saw Archie*
_____ 10 *A Face in the Crowd* and *The Fountainhead*
_____ 11 *Double Indemnity* and *Sorry, Wrong Number*
_____ 12 *Beau Brummel* and *National Velvet*

a Lilli Palmer
b Barbara Stanwyck
c Dirk Bogarde
d Joan Bennett
e Robert Mitchum
f Eddie Albert
g Patricia Neal
h Robert Redford
i Joel McCrea
j Elizabeth Taylor
k Eve Arden
l Tyrone Power

_____ **Score**
(5 points each)

The Ph.D. Level

_____ 1 *Key Largo* and *Murder My Sweet*
_____ 2 *The Thin Man* and *The Bachelor and the Bobby Soxer*
_____ 3 *Houdini* and *Rogue Cop*
_____ 4 *The Manchurian Candidate* and *State of the Union*
_____ 5 *The Glass Menagerie* and *Nevada Smith*
_____ 6 *Lolita* and *A Place in the Sun*
_____ 7 *The Spiral Staircase* and *Dark Victory*
_____ 8 *Captain from Castile* and *Twelve Angry Men*
_____ 9 *The Uninvited* and *Dawn Patrol*
_____ 10 *The War Lord* and *The Kremlin Letter*
_____ 11 *The Kid from Left Field* and *The Slender Thread*
_____ 12 *Son of Frankenstein* and *Captain Blood*

a Donald Crisp
b Angela Lansbury
c Anne Bancroft
d Shelley Winters
e Lee J. Cobb
f Myrna Loy
g Janet Leigh
h Richard Boone
i Arthur Kennedy
j Lionel Atwill
k Claire Trevor
l George Brent

_____ **Score**
(5 points each)

Test 93

Baseball Cards—Collector's Items

Collecting baseball cards has been the hobby of kids for a long time. The most valuable card is of Honus Wagner, who didn't believe in smoking and demanded successfully that cards with his picture be withdrawn from circulation, and only a few have survived. Surely card collectors can match each of the following players with one of the teams for which they played (but not always the one with which they are most associated.)

The B.A. Level

____ **1** Harvey Kuenn	**a** Chicago White Sox
____ **2** Early Wynn	**b** Boston Red Sox
____ **3** Bob Kennedy	**c** San Francisco Giants
____ **4** Satchel Paige	**d** Milwaukee Brewers
____ **5** Lou Brock	**e** Kansas City Royals
____ **6** Maury Wills	**f** Washington Senators
____ **7** Roy McMillan	**g** Pittsburgh Pirates
____ **8** Hank Aaron	**h** St. Louis Browns
____ **9** Lou Pinella	**i** New York Mets
____ **10** Bob Watson	**j** Chicago Cubs

________ **Score**
(5 points each)

The M.S. Level

____ **1** Ron Reed	**a** Houston Astros
____ **2** Ron Hansen	**b** Brooklyn Dodgers
____ **3** Dick Farrell	**c** Atlanta Braves
____ **4** Ben Ogilvie	**d** New York Giants
____ **5** Hank Sauer	**e** Minnesota Twins
____ **6** Red Schoendienst	**f** Texas Rangers
____ **7** Andy Pafko	**g** Cleveland Indians
____ **8** Elliott Maddox	**h** Milwaukee Braves
____ **9** Billy Martin	**i** Chicago White Sox
____ **10** Herb Score	**j** Boston Red Sox

________ **Score**
(5 points each)

The Ph.D. Level

____ **1** Mort Cooper	**a** Los Angeles Angels
____ **2** John Podres	**b** Boston Red Sox
____ **3** Bobo Newson	**c** Philadelphia Phillies
____ **4** Steve Bilko	**d** Detroit Tigers
____ **5** Cal McLish	**e** Seattle Pilots
____ **6** Solly Hemus	**f** Boston Braves
____ **7** Don Hoak	**g** New York Yankees
____ **8** Tommy Davis	**h** Washington Senators
____ **9** Dick Stuart	**i** Cleveland Indians
____ **10** Enos Slaughter	**j** Cincinnati Reds

________ **Score**
(5 points each)

Test 94

Broadway Musicals—Of Thee I Sing—A Reprise

Match the following songs with the Broadway musicals in which they were featured.

The B.A. Level

_____ **1** "My Darlin' Eileen"
_____ **2** "Indian Love Call"
_____ **3** "Once in a Lifetime"
_____ **4** "Tell Me, Pretty Maiden"
_____ **5** "I Could Write a Book"
_____ **6** "I Ain't Down Yet"
_____ **7** "One Last Kiss"
_____ **8** "There But for You, Go I"
_____ **9** "Try to Remember"
_____ **10** "Molasses to Rum"
_____ **11** "What a Piece of Work is Man"
_____ **12** "Every day is Ladies' Day with Me"

a *Florodora*
b *The Fantasticks*
c *Bye, Bye, Birdie*
d *The Unsinkable Molly Brown*
e *Rose Marie*
f *The Red Mill*
g *Hair*
h *Wonderful Town*
i *"1776"*
j *Stop the World—I Want to Get Off*
k *Pal Joey*
l *Brigadoon*

__________ **Score**
(5 points each)

The M.S. Level

_____ **1** "Stan' Up and Fight"
_____ **2** "Softly, As in a Morning Sunrise"
_____ **3** "Some Day"
_____ **4** "The Best Things in Life Are Free"
_____ **5** "I'll Never Fall in Love Again"
_____ **6** "Once in Love with Amy"
_____ **7** "As Long as He Needs Me"
_____ **8** "How Are Things in Glocca Morra?"
_____ **9** "Namely You"
_____ **10** "Tomorrow Belongs to Me"
_____ **11** "Love, Look Away"
_____ **12** "Night of My Nights"

a *The New Moon*
b *Kismet*
c *Where's Charley*
d *Carmen Jones*
e *Flower Drum Song*
f *Li'l Abner*
g *The Vagabond King*
h *Cabaret*
i *Good News*
j *Promises, Promises*
k *Finian's Rainbow*
l *Oliver!*

__________ **Score**
(5 points each)

The Ph.D. Level

_____ **1** "Alice Blue Gown"
_____ **2** "After the Ball"
_____ **3** "T'morra, T'morra"
_____ **4** "Blues in the Night"
_____ **5** "Bright College Days"
_____ **6** "Three Little Maids"
_____ **7** "Love Makes the World Go"
_____ **8** "My Cup Runneth Over"
_____ **9** "Close as Pages in a Book"
_____ **10** "Yankee Dollar"
_____ **11** "Speak Low"
_____ **12** "Look for the Silver Lining"

a *No Strings*
b *Blossom Time*
c *Jamaica*
d *A Trip to Chinatown*
e *Irene*
f *I Do! I Do!*
g *One Touch of Venus*
h *Bloomer Girl*
i *Sally*
j *Up in Central Park*
k *Star and Garter*
l *Wish You Were Here*

__________ **Score**
(5 points each)

Test 95

Who Said That?—Movies of the Fifties

Here are some memorable quotes from movies of the fifties. Match the quotes with the characters, the actors who portrayed them, and the movie the quote is taken from.

The B.A. Level

___|___ **1** "Fasten your seat belts, it's going to be a bumpy night."

___|___ **2** "You are unworthy of command."

___|___ **3** "So what happens? He gets the title shot outdoors in the ballpark. And what do I get? A one-way ticket to Palookaville."

___|___ **4** "Go with him; Madge, for once in your life, do something bright."

___|___ **5** "You just gotta marry me, future or no future."

___|___ **6** "Hello, everybody—this is—Mrs. Norman Maine."

___|___ **7** "We didn't need dialogue. We had faces then."

___|___ **8** "I'll cook and I'll work and I'll keep the land. But that is all—until I've got my dowry."

___|___ **9** "I cry a lot too. I'm a big crier. I know exactly how you feel."

___|___ **10** "So sorry, but I had to leave suddenly. I was seized by an irresistible impulse."

a Marty Pilletti
b Norma Desmond
c Frederick Manion
d Alice Tripp
e Mary Kate Danaher
f Colonel Saito
g Terry Malloy
h Vicki Lestor
i Margo Channing
j Millie Owens

I Gloria Swanson *(Sunset Boulevard)*
II Shelley Winters *(A Place in the Sun)*
III Susan Strasberg *(Picnic)*
IV Ernest Borgnine *(Marty)*
V Judy Garland *(A Star is Born)*
VI Bette Davis *(All About Eve)*
VII Sessue Hayakawa *(The Bridge Over the River Kwai)*
VIII Maureen O'Hara *(The Quiet Man)*
IX Marlon Brando *(On the Waterfront)*
X Ben Gazzara *(Anatomy of a Murder)*

________**Score**
(5 points each)

The M.S. Level

___|___ **1** "F'heaven's sake, what's the idea? Can't a girl get a word in edgewise?"

___|___ **2** "It's not Mrs. Brock. There ain't no Mrs. Brock except my mother. And she's dead."

___|___ **3** "But I proved beyond the shadow of a doubt and with geometric logic that a duplicate key to the ward room icebox did exist."

___|___ **4** "We've had this date with each other from the beginning."

___|___ **5** "You better give me something, Dad, you better give me something fast, Dad, stand up for me."

___|___ **6** "When I'm with a girl, it does absolutely nothing to me. No feelings. Like my heart is shot full of novocaine."

___|___ **7** "Guys like you end up in the stockade sooner or later. I'll be waiting."

___|___ **8** "It's no good, I've got to go back, Amy."

___|___ **9** "If there's anything worse than a woman living alone, it's a woman saying she likes it."

___|___ **10** "My immaculate wife, I thought you were everything good and pure. I'd rather go to jail for twenty years than find out my wife was a tramp."

a Harry Brock
b James McLeod
c Stanley Kowalski
d Jim Stark
e Captain Queeg
f Alma
g Will Kane
h Joe
i Lina Lamont
j Fatso Judson

I Marlon Brando *(A Streetcar Named Desire)*
II Tony Curtis *(Some Like It Hot)*
III Ernest Borgnine *(From Here to Eternity)*
IV Kirk Douglas *(Detective Story)*
V Jean Hagen *(Singin' in the Rain)*
VI Humphrey Bogart *(The Caine Mutiny)*
VII Thelma Ritter *(Pillow Talk)*
VIII Gary Cooper *(High Noon)*
IX Broderick Crawford *(Born Yesterday)*
X James Dean *(Rebel Without a Cause)*

________**Score**
(5 points each)

Test 95

The Ph.D. Level

____ **1** "Because he drank, you're a drunk, because he loved women, you're a tramp."

____ **2** "You ever try to fight thirty-five guys at one time, Teach?"

____ **3** "It is said that no man is a hero to his valet. It's also true that no woman is a mystery to her husband's valet."

____ **4** "A man's life ain't worth a hill of beans—except he lives up to his conscience. I've got to give Josh his chance."

____ **5** "They'll all die violently—the spies, the liars, all the others who want me dead. I'm innocent."

____ **6** "Monkey's never dead and monkey never dies. You kick him off. He just hides in a corner waiting his turn."

____ **7** "There are few things more fundamentally encouraging and stimulating than seeing someone else die."

____ **8** "Darling, you're crying, I believe you're really sentimental after all."

____ **9** "We're all prisoners of each other's gossip, killed by each other's whispers."

____ **10** "There's no pain. Suddenly, while you're asleep, they'll absorb your minds, your memories. And you'll be reborn into an untroubled world."

____ **Score**
(5 points each)

a Jess Birdwell
b Dr. Dan Kaufman
c Artie West
d General Broulard
e Louie
f Dr. Mathew Swain
g Jonathan Shields
h Cicero
i Barbara Graham
j Susan Brown

I Susan Hayward *(I Want to Live!)*
II Heather Sears *(Room at the Top)*
III James Mason *(Five Fingers)*
IV Kirk Douglas *(The Bad and the Beautiful)*
V Darren McGavin *(The Man With the Golden Arm)*
VI Lloyd Nolan *(Peyton Place)*
VII Gary Cooper *(Friendly Persuasion)*
VIII Vic Morrow *(The Blackboard Jungle)*
IX Adolphe Menjou *(Paths of Glory)*
X Larry Gates *(Invasion of the Body Snatchers)*

Test 96

Song Titles—A Musical Potpourri

Match the songs with their first lines. In this test there is no theme—just some fine songs.

The B.A. Level

____ **1**	"Come and meet these dancing feet . . ."	**a**	"In My Merry Oldsmobile"
____ **2**	"If you miss the train I'm on . . ."	**b**	"Forty-Second Street"
____ **3**	"A law was made a distant moon ago here . . ."	**c**	"My Heart Stood Still"
____ **4**	"No one to talk with, all by myself . . ."	**d**	"Tea for Two"
____ **5**	"Trailer for sale or rent . . ."	**e**	"Don't Fence Me In"
____ **6**	"She comes down from Yellow Mountain . . ."	**f**	"As Time Goes By"
____ **7**	"Picture you upon my knee . . ."	**g**	"Five Hundred Miles"
____ **8**	"Oh, give me land, lots of land . . ."	**h**	"Let's Do It!"
____ **9**	"You must remember this, a kiss is just a kiss . . ."	**i**	"Camelot"
____ **10**	"Come away with me, Lucille . . ."	**j**	"Ain't Misbehavin'"
____ **11**	"Birds do it, bees do it . . ."	**k**	"King of the Road"
____ **12**	"I took one look at you . . ."	**l**	"Wildfire"

________ **Score**
(5 points each)

The M.S. Level

____ **1**	"There is somebody I'm longing to see . . ."	**a**	"It Was a Very Good Year"
____ **2**	"The old hometown looks the same . . ."	**b**	"Twilight Time"
____ **3**	"East is east and west is west . . ."	**c**	"Friendship"
____ **4**	"No gal made has got a shade . . ."	**d**	"Autumn Leaves"
____ **5**	"Oh, the shark has pretty teeth, dear . . ."	**e**	"Games People Play"
____ **6**	"Someday, he'll come along . . ."	**f**	"The Boxer"
____ **7**	"The falling leaves drift by the window . . ."	**g**	"Someone to Watch Over Me"
____ **8**	"When I was seventeen . . ."	**h**	"Green Green Grass of Home"
____ **9**	"I am just a poor boy . . ."	**i**	"Mack the Knife"
____ **10**	"If you're ever in a jam . . ."	**j**	"Buttons and Bows"
____ **11**	"Talkin' about you and me . . ."	**k**	"The Man I Love"
____ **12**	"Heavenly shades of night are falling . . ."	**l**	"Sweet Georgia Brown"

________ **Score**
(5 points each)

The Ph.D. Level

____ **1**	"You live your life in songs you hear . . ."	**a**	"A Horse With No Name"
____ **2**	"My mama done tol' me, when I was in knee-pants . . ."	**b**	"Rock 'n' Roll Heaven"
____ **3**	"We're in the money . . ."	**c**	"The Heather on the Hill"
____ **4**	"Oh the first part of the journey . . ."	**d**	"The Birth of the Blues"
____ **5**	"They say we're young and we don't know . . ."	**e**	"Blues in the Night"
____ **6**	"You ask me if there'll come a time . . ."	**f**	"Cast Your Fate to the Wind"
____ **7**	"If you believe in heaven . . ."	**g**	"Ain't That a Shame"
____ **8**	"Ain't no lions or tigers ain't no mamba snakes . . ."	**h**	"I Got You, Babe"
____ **9**	"A month of nights, a year of days . . ."	**i**	"Angie Baby"
____ **10**	"This mist of May in the gloamin' . . ."	**j**	"Never, My Love"
____ **11**	"You made me cry when you said goodbye . . ."	**k**	"Sail Away"
____ **12**	"They heard the breeze in the trees . . ."	**l**	"The Gold Digger's Song"

________ **Score**
(5 points each)

Test 97

What's in a Name—A Reprise

Once again, match the character from a musical with the show.

The B.A. Level

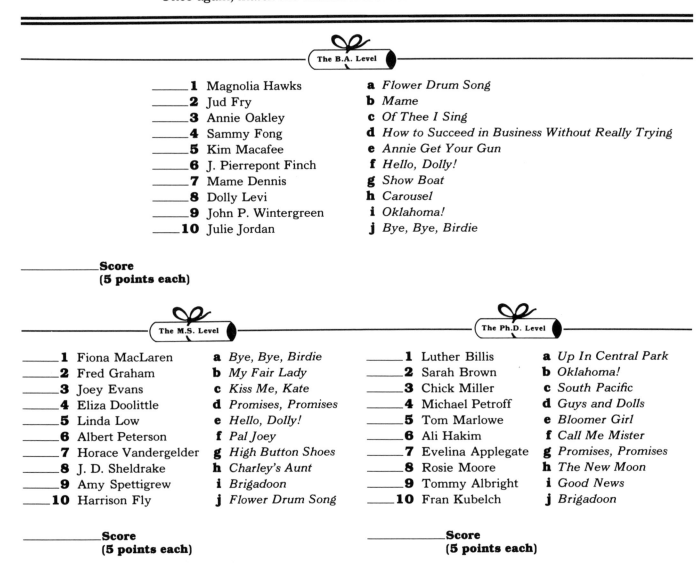

____ **1** Magnolia Hawks	**a** *Flower Drum Song*
____ **2** Jud Fry	**b** *Mame*
____ **3** Annie Oakley	**c** *Of Thee I Sing*
____ **4** Sammy Fong	**d** *How to Succeed in Business Without Really Trying*
____ **5** Kim Macafee	**e** *Annie Get Your Gun*
____ **6** J. Pierrepont Finch	**f** *Hello, Dolly!*
____ **7** Mame Dennis	**g** *Show Boat*
____ **8** Dolly Levi	**h** *Carousel*
____ **9** John P. Wintergreen	**i** *Oklahoma!*
____ **10** Julie Jordan	**j** *Bye, Bye, Birdie*

________ **Score**
(5 points each)

The M.S. Level

____ **1** Fiona MacLaren	**a** *Bye, Bye, Birdie*
____ **2** Fred Graham	**b** *My Fair Lady*
____ **3** Joey Evans	**c** *Kiss Me, Kate*
____ **4** Eliza Doolittle	**d** *Promises, Promises*
____ **5** Linda Low	**e** *Hello, Dolly!*
____ **6** Albert Peterson	**f** *Pal Joey*
____ **7** Horace Vandergelder	**g** *High Button Shoes*
____ **8** J. D. Sheldrake	**h** *Charley's Aunt*
____ **9** Amy Spettigrew	**i** *Brigadoon*
____ **10** Harrison Fly	**j** *Flower Drum Song*

________ **Score**
(5 points each)

The Ph.D. Level

____ **1** Luther Billis	**a** *Up In Central Park*
____ **2** Sarah Brown	**b** *Oklahoma!*
____ **3** Chick Miller	**c** *South Pacific*
____ **4** Michael Petroff	**d** *Guys and Dolls*
____ **5** Tom Marlowe	**e** *Bloomer Girl*
____ **6** Ali Hakim	**f** *Call Me Mister*
____ **7** Evelina Applegate	**g** *Promises, Promises*
____ **8** Rosie Moore	**h** *The New Moon*
____ **9** Tommy Albright	**i** *Good News*
____ **10** Fran Kubelch	**j** *Brigadoon*

________ **Score**
(5 points each)

Test 98

A Literary Collection

If you have been a good student of dear Old College of Trivial Knowledge, you spent a great deal of time in the library and should be able to identify each of the following books.

The B.A. Level

_____**1** account of Woodrow Wilson's last years in the presidency
_____**2** a plea for greater urgency and common sense on the issue of civil rights
_____**3** an urban intellectual's efforts to find himself in a world not of his making
_____**4** on the weird and wonderful inhabitants of St. Botolphs
_____**5** the spiritual odyssey of the late Secretary-General of the U.N.
_____**6** an indictment of the Vatican as morally responsible for the death of six million Jews
_____**7** superlative collection of tales of Eastern European Jewish life
_____**8** an allegorical novel on the theme "Should a man's reach exceed his grasp"
_____**9** poetry celebrating the wonders of nature and the dignity of life
_____**10** ironic short stories, ranging from sketches of life in Colorado to life in prewar Germany

a *The Far Field*
b *The Wapshot Chronicle*
c *Why We Can't Wait*
d *Short Friday*
e *Bad Characters*
f *When the Cheering Stopped*
g *The Spire*
h *Herzog*
i *The Deputy*
j *Markings*

_____**Score**
(5 points each)

The M.S. Level

_____**1** portrait of an independent and stubborn old woman clinging to the last vestiges of human dignity
_____**2** a master chess strategist's difficulties in making the proper moves in his personal life
_____**3** precise and elegant poetry of the problems of modern times
_____**4** absorbing account of the conflicts between the courts and justice for the poor man
_____**5** recreation of Shakespeare's life as he may have lived it
_____**6** bizarre tale of an eccentric family and their amorous encounters
_____**7** account of the Burke-Wills expedition through the Australian interior
_____**8** unorthodox historical survey of dissenters against the social conventions of their times
_____**9** fictional evocation of childhood experiences with life and death
_____**10** scientist's inspired account of a life dedicated to research

a *The Italian Girl*
b *From Dream to Discovery*
c *The Defense*
d *Things As They Are*
e *Heroes and Heretics*
f *The Stone Angel*
g *Nothing Like the Sun*
h *For the Union Dead*
i *Cooper's Creek*
j *Gideon's Trumpet*

_____**Score**
(5 points each)

Test 98

The Ph.D. Level

_____ **1** a metaphorical fugue on minds and machines
_____ **2** moving depiction of Irish life in the time of troubles
_____ **3** thirteen billion years of the universe's evolution
_____ **4** life in occupied France geographically portrayed by a Scotswoman
_____ **5** one hundred ordinary men and women talk about their hopes and fears
_____ **6** tender and sympathetic novel on the theme of man's moral responsibility to man
_____ **7** prescription for "achieving perfection of body and mind"
_____ **8** why the world did not hear of Hitler's "final solution" until after World War II
_____ **9** guide for job hunters and career changers
_____ **10** biographical novel of Charles Darwin

a *Divided Loyalties*
b *The Origin*
c *The Sky's The Limit*
d *Gödel, Escher, Bach*
e *The Tears Might Cease*
f *American Dreams*
g *Cosmos*
h *What Color Is Your Parachute?*
i *Children at the Gate*
j *The Terrible Secret*

_____ **Score**
(5 points each)

Test 99

The End of Potpourri

The B.A. Level

1.________________ The breaking of some small figurines creates a dramatic scene in the play . . .

2.________________ Who was Aristotle's teacher?

3.________________ The book *Ben and Me,* by Robert Lawson, is a story about . . .

4.________________ What was the name of the 6-inch-high Kleenex Napkins' TV butler?

5.________________ Whose portrait appears on a $100,000 bill?

6.________________ In *Cyrano de Bergerac,* Christian is killed by . . .

7.________________ What role did lawyer Joseph Welch play in *Anatomy of a Murder*?

8.________________ What was the scarlet letter?

9.________________ Who is the patron saint of Ireland?

10.________________ Who played George Plimpton in the movie *Paper Lion*?

__________**Score**
(5 points each)

The M.S. Level

1.________________ What was the name of the TV character who said, "Is this the party to whom I am speaking?"

2.________________ What university did Frank Merriwell attend?

3.________________ What movie was advertised with the slogan, "Gable's back and Garson's got him"?

4.________________ What is the name of the intellectual buzzard friend of Broom-Hilda, the witch?

5.________________ What was the name of the ship on which Charles Darwin made his scientific voyage?

6.________________ What was the character played by Tim Conway on *McHale's Navy*?

7.________________ What was Clinton's Folly?

8.________________ What was the name of the commander of Fort Apache in the movie of that name, played by Henry Fonda?

9.________________ Who usually said, "You're looking fine, Riley, very natural"?

10.________________ Who was the founder of Christian Science?

__________**Score**
(5 points each)

The Ph.D. Level

1.________________ Who played the clown Buttons in the movie *The Greatest Show on Earth?*

2.________________ Savonarola appears as a character in . . .

3.________________ What was the name of Sir Thomas Lipton's yachts in his attempts to win the American Cup?

4.________________ What is the traditional food served each year at Wimbledon?

5.________________ What was the name of Carrie Nation's newspaper?

6.________________ What was the name of the Cunard lines ship torpedoed and sunk in 1915 off the coast of Ireland?

7.________________ What does onomatopoeia mean?

8.________________ The symbol "&" is called . . .

9.________________ What is a Cadmean victory?

10.________________ What squares in the British version of monopoly correspond to Park Place and Boardwalk?

__________**Score**
(5 points each)

Test **100**

An International Banquet

Now that you have completed your studies at dear old College of Trivial Knowledge, it is fitting and proper that you participate in a great celebration. The tables are laden with food from all over the world. For your final test, identify what you are eating.

The B.A. Level

____ **1** Escalopes de Veau Panées	**a** a dish of melted or toasted cheese
____ **2** Borscht	**b** cookies immortalized by Marcel Proust
____ **3** Moussaka	**c** chicken with rice
____ **4** Welsh Rarebit	**d** steak marinated in soy sauce
____ **5** Madeleines	**e** beet soup
____ **6** Carbonnades à la Flamande	**f** scallop soup
____ **7** Teriyaki	**g** fish soup or broth
____ **8** Crème St. Jacques	**h** breaded veal scallops
____ **9** Coq au Vin	**i** a beef stew made with beer
____ **10** Bouillabaisse	**j** meat and eggplant dish

________ **Score**
(5 points each)

The M.S. Level

____ **1** Paskha	**a** jellied pork loaf
____ **2** Hallacas	**b** mussel soup
____ **3** Suimono	**c** lamb and parsley stew
____ **4** Schweinsulze	**d** Chilean meat turnovers
____ **5** Hassenpfeffer	**e** Russian pot cheese desert
____ **6** Gormeh Sabzee	**f** pork pie
____ **7** Empanadas	**g** roasted rabbit
____ **8** Billi Bi	**h** an Armenian hors d'oeuvre
____ **9** Plaky	**i** Venezuelan version of tamales
____ **10** Tourtière	**j** a plain soup made with bonito

________ **Score**
(5 points each)

The Ph.D. Level

____ **1** Bollito Misto	**a** spiced breast of veal
____ **2** Chorizo	**b** Greek butter cookies
____ **3** Rullepolse	**c** sauerkraut with meats
____ **4** Pirozhki	**d** Pakistani cocktail made with yogurt
____ **5** Borani	**e** Italian seafood stew
____ **6** Kourambiedes	**f** a mixed boil—everything in the pot
____ **7** Cacciucco	**g** Spanish hot sausage
____ **8** Pastel de Choclo	**h** Greek roast leg of lamb
____ **9** Arni Psito	**i** Russian meat turnovers
____ **10** Choucroute à l'Alsacienne	**j** Chilean casserole

________ **Score**
(5 points each)

Answers

Test 1:

The B.A. Level

1-c	6-d
2-i	7-h
3-g	8-j
4-e	9-f
5-b	10-a

The M.S. Level

1-d	6-h
2-e	7-a
3-g	8-b
4-f	9-j
5-i	10-c

The Ph.D. Level

1-h	6-b
2-d	7-j
3-i	8-c
4-a	9-g
5-e	10-f

Test 2:

The B.A. Level

1-g	6-b
2-d	7-i
3-e	8-c
4-a	9-f
5-j	10-h

The M.S. Level

1-j	6-d
2-e	7-a
3-b	8-g
4-f	9-c
5-h	10-i

The Ph.D. Level

1-b	6-d
2-e	7-h
3-j	8-f
4-i	9-c
5-a	10-g

Test 3:

The B.A. Level

1 William Henry Harrison
2 Benjamin Harrison
3 Theodore Roosevelt
4 Richard M. Nixon
5 Lyndon B. Johnson
6 James Buchanan
7 John Quincy Adams
8 John F. Kennedy
9 Ronald W. Reagan
10 William Howard Taft

The M.S. Level

1 Herbert C. Hoover
2 Dwight D. Eisenhower
3 Andrew Johnson
4 James Madison
5 Abraham Lincoln
6 Franklin Pierce
7 Harry S Truman
8 Woodrow Wilson
9 Calvin Coolidge
10 Martin Van Buren

The Ph.D. Level

1 James Knox Polk
2 Andrew Jackson
3 James Monroe
4 Ulysses S. Grant
5 Warren G. Harding
6 Franklin D. Roosevelt
7 Thomas Jefferson
8 Millard Fillmore
9 Zachary Taylor
10 Grover Cleveland

Test 4:

The B.A. Level

1-d	6-g
2-f	7-h
3-a	8-j
4-i	9-e
5-b	10-c

The M.S. Level

1-b	6-a
2-i	7-h
3-f	8-d
4-e	9-c
5-j	10-g

The Ph.D. Level

1-e	6-i
2-a	7-h
3-f	8-j
4-d	9-g
5-c	10-b

Test 5:

The B.A. Level

1 Gepetto
2 "My Day"
3 danger from pesticides
4 Clydesdale
5 Simon Legree
6 Lucky Strike
7 Benjamin Franklin
8 *The House at Pooh Corner*
9 Leo G. Carroll
10 Mel Blanc

The M.S. Level

1 The Grinch
2 Monticello
3 Edward Jenner
4 drank poison hemlock
5 Noel Coward
6 Colonel Rudolf Abel
7 Clara Barton
8 Clermont
9 Jacob Morley
10 Digger Phelps

The Ph.D. Level

1 St. Andrew
2 Service Above Self
3 Henry
4 Christian Huygens
5 Joel Chandler Harris
6 a song of mourning
7 *Crime and Punishment*
8 *Abbey Road*
9 July 14
10 the original Siamese twins

Test 6:

The B.A. Level

1-e	6-j
2-i	7-c
3-a	8-b
4-g	9-f
5-d	10-h

The M.S. Level

1-c	6-a
2-j	7-b
3-i	8-e
4-g	9-d
5-f	10-h

The Ph.D. Level

1-b	6-j
2-i	7-e
3-d	8-c
4-g	9-h
5-f	10-a

Test 7:

The B.A. Level

1-h	6-b
2-f	7-j
3-e	8-d
4-i	9-g
5-c	10-a

The M.S. Level

1-h	6-a
2-e	7-g
3-b	8-c
4-i	9-f
5-j	10-d

The Ph.D. Level

1-f	6-a
2-d	7-i
3-g	8-j
4-e	9-h
5-c	10-b

Test 8:

The B.A. Level

1-g	7-i
2-k	8-c
3-e	9-f
4-b	10-d
5-l	11-j
6-a	12-h

The M.S. Level

1-d	7-a
2-i	8-j
3-h	9-e
4-k	10-g
5-b	11-f
6-l	12-c

The Ph.D. Level

1-j	7-d
2-f	8-k
3-a	9-g
4-b	10-i
5-h	11-c
6-l	12-e

Test 9:

The B.A. Level

1-j	7-l
2-d	8-f
3-g	9-e
4-a	10-h
5-k	11-c
6-b	12-i

The M.S. Level

1-c	7-l
2-e	8-k
3-f	9-h
4-i	10-g
5-b	11-a
6-j	12-d

The Ph.D. Level

1-l	7-c
2-d	8-k
3-a	9-j
4-f	10-i
5-b	11-g
6-h	12-e

Test 10:

The B.A. Level

1 Ronald Reagan
2 Kings
3 Phoenix Suns
4 Meadowlark Lemon
5 Glenn Ford
6 Chicago Cubs
7 second base
8 home run with bases loaded
9 9–0
10 none, did not participate

The M.S. Level

1 Chicago White Sox
2 third base
3 Ralph Kiner
4 15 feet
5 Jack Sharkey
6 Pelé
7 a driver
8 covers the middle section of the field
9 The Downtown Athletic Club
10 1968

The Ph.D. Level

1 *My Turn at Bat*
2 Bret Hanover
3 the U.S.S.R.
4 Burleigh Grimes
5 Luis Aparicio
6 Glenn "Pop" Warner
7 Mike Bossy
8 Steve Vickers
9 Ken Buchanan
10 Montclair State College

Test 11:

The B.A. Level

1-g	6-b
2-c	7-e
3-f	8-j
4-a	9-h
5-i	10-d

The M.S. Level

1-b	6-j
2-f	7-c
3-e	8-g
4-h	9-i
5-a	10-d

The Ph.D. Level

1-c	6-a
2-g	7-e
3-d	8-j
4-h	9-f
5-i	10-b

Test 12:

The B.A. Level

1-g	9-o
2-k	10-a
3-j	11-c
4-m	12-h
5-n	13-i
6-d	14-f
7-e	15-l
8-b	

The M.S. Level

1-m	9-f
2-j	10-g
3-i	11-h
4-o	12-n
5-a	13-e
6-d	14-k
7-c	15-l
8-b	

The Ph.D. Level

1-j	9-g
2-e	10-f
3-b	11-c
4-m	12-n
5-h	13-o
6-a	14-l
7-k	15-i
8-d	

Test 13:

The B.A. Level

1-f	6-g
2-i	7-e
3-h	8-b
4-j	9-d
5-a	10-c

The M.S. Level

1-j	6-d
2-f	7-i
3-h	8-e
4-b	9-a
5-c	10-g

The Ph.D. Level

1-d	6-b
2-h	7-c
3-i	8-e
4-j	9-f
5-a	10-g

Test 14:

The B.A. Level

1-d	7-e
2-j	8-a
3-g	9-l
4-h	10-i
5-b	11-f
6-k	12-c

The M.S. Level

1-l	7-a
2-d	8-b
3-i	9-g
4-k	10-h
5-j	11-f
6-c	12-e

The Ph.D. Level

1-j	7-l
2-f	8-k
3-a	9-d
4-g	10-c
5-b	11-h
6-i	12-e

Test 15:

The B.A. Level

1 butcher
2 Jett Rink
3 Kirk Douglas
4 *Sincerely Yours*
5 *The Silver Chalice*
6 Margaret O'Brien
7 Marjorie Main
8 Marlon Brando
9 Joan Fontaine and Olivia De Havilland
10 Lon Chaney

The M.S. Level

1 George Macready
2 Kim Stanley
3 Mickey Rooney
4 Strother Martin
5 *Anna Christie*
6 Alexander Knox
7 a crop duster
8 Cedric Hardwicke
9 court executioner
10 *Buck Privates*

The Ph.D. Level

1 Rex Ingram
2 Valerie Hobson
3 Knobby Walsh
4 Robert Blake
5 John Clayton, Lord Greystoke
6 *Duck Soup*
7 Cantinflas
8 Priscilla Lane
9 George Arliss
10 *Go Into Your Dance*

Test 16:

The B.A. Level

1 Peace Corps
2 Timothy Leary
3 Martin Luther King, Jr.
4 Rhythm method
5 *Armies of the Night*
6 Jimmy Hoffa
7 Muhammad Ali
8 John Lennon
9 Bay of Pigs
10 payola

The M.S. Level

1 The U-2 flights over U.S.S.R.
2 Bill Russell–Boston Celtics
3 Caryl Chessman
4 Thomas Dodd of Connecticut
5 China
6 *Citizen Kane*
7 *Unsafe at Any Speed*
8 Abe Fortas
9 Eugene McCarthy
10 The United Auto Workers

The Ph.D. Level

1 Haight-Ashbury
2 Richard Speck
3 Telstar
4 Stokely Carmichael
5 Adam Clayton Powell
6 Pueblo
7 *Aristotle Contemplating the Bust of Homer*
8 James Meredith
9 barred poll taxes in federal elections
10 Robert Weaver of HUD

Test 17:

The B.A. Level

1 improvise
2 verse
3 field hollers
4 chamber music
5 jam session
6 round
7 chorus
8 gospel songs
9 standard tunes
10 combo

The M.S. Level

1 hymn
2 Storyville
3 tempo
4 quadrille
5 harmony
6 liturgical
7 syncopation
8 spiritual
9 melody
10 sideman

The Ph.D. Level

1 vibrato
2 riff
3 ostinato
4 cross-rhythm
5 flatted tone
6 rondo
7 pedal point
8 vamp
9 well-tempered scale
10 sharped tone

Test 18:

The B.A. Level

1-g	6-b
2-c	7-e
3-j	8-f
4-a	9-h
5-i	10-d

The M.S. Level

1-d	6-h
2-i	7-b
3-a	8-c
4-g	9-f
5-j	10-e

The Ph.D. Level

1-d	6-e
2-a	7-j
3-h	8-i
4-b	9-f
5-g	10-c

Test 19:

The B.A. Level

1-c	6-b
2-g	7-j
3-a	8-e
4-i	9-f
5-h	10-d

The M.S. Level

1-b	6-g
2-e	7-j
3-a	8-f
4-h	9-c
5-d	10-i

The Ph.D. Level

1-e	6-j
2-f	7-d
3-b	8-g
4-i	9-c
5-h	10-a

Test 20:

The B.A. Level

1 Nashville, Tenn.
2 B. F. Goodrich
3 Don MacNeil
4 John Bull
5 Rollo
6 Roy Earle
7 Major Edward Bowes
8 Polly Adler
9 Grace Kelly
10 *Anthony Adverse*

The M.S. Level

1 17 years
2 Willie and Joe
3 for this purpose
4 a number exactly divisible only by itself and one
5 Minnehaha
6 Claude Kirchner
7 Arthur Shields
8 Oveta Culp Hobby
9 *Tommy*
10 Abigail Van Buren

The Ph.D. Level

1 the Portuguese river northwest of Lisbon
2 *The Chocolate Soldier*
3 Abraham Zapruder
4 Sonia
5 Oberlin College
6 Voltaire's *Candide*
7 efficiency experts
8 Edna St. Vincent Millay
9 *Washington Square*
10 bibliopegy

Test 21:

The B.A. Level

1 Bette Davis—*The Petrified Forest*
2 Joan Crawford—*Rain*
3 Joan Crawford—*Humoresque*
4 Barbara Stanwyck—*Double Indemnity*
5 Bette Davis—*Jezebel*
6 Bette Davis—*Juarez*
7 Barbara Stanwyck—*Stella Dallas*
8 Joan Crawford—*The Gorgeous Hussy*
9 Barbara Stanwyck—*Christmas in Connecticut*
10 Barbara Stanwyck—*Golden Boy*
11 Joan Crawford—*Flamingo Road*
12 Bette Davis—*Of Human Bondage*

The M.S. Level

1 Barbara Stanwyck—*Lady of Burlesque*
2 Barbara Stanwyck—*The Strange Love of Martha Ivers*
3 Bette Davis—*The Corn Is Green*
4 Joan Crawford—*Mildred Pierce*
5 Joan Crawford—*Harriet Craig*
6 Bette Davis—*Now, Voyager*
7 Bette Davis—*The Little Foxes*
8 Joan Crawford—*This Woman is Dangerous*
9 Barbara Stanwyck—*The Gay Sisters*
10 Barbara Stanwyck—*Meet John Doe*
11 Bette Davis—*Dangerous*
12 Joan Crawford—*Daisy Kenyon*

The Ph.D. Level

1 Joan Crawford—*The Bride Wore Red*
2 Joan Crawford—*Sudden Fear*
3 Barbara Stanwyck—*The Lady Eve*
4 Bette Davis—*The Old Maid*
5 Bette Davis—*Dark Victory*
6 Bette Davis—*Mr. Skeffington*
7 Barbara Stanwyck—*The Furies*
8 Barbara Stanwyck—*Ball of Fire*
9 Bette Davis—*A Stolen Life*
10 Joan Crawford—*The Story of Esther Costello*
11 Barbara Stanwyck—*The Two Mrs. Carrolls*
12 Joan Crawford—*Possessed*

Test 22:

The B.A. Level

1-e	6-a
2-h	7-b
3-i	8-c
4-j	9-f
5-d	10-g

The M.S. Level

1-c	6-h
2-i	7-f
3-j	8-e
4-g	9-a
5-b	10-d

The Ph.D. Level

1-f	6-j
2-c	7-e
3-h	8-b
4-a	9-g
5-i	10-d

Test 23:

The B.A. Level

1 swimming
2 figure skating
3 golf
4 gymnastics
5 boxing
6 baseball
7 track and field
8 football
9 tennis
10 track and field

The M.S. Level

1 golf
2 tennis
3 baseball
4 swimming
5 football
6 golf
7 gymnastics
8 boxing
9 golf
10 horse racing

The Ph.D. Level

1 track and field
2 diving
3 swimming
4 tennis
5 track and field
6 tennis
7 golf
8 track and field
9 golf
10 swimming

Test 24:

The B.A. Level

1-d	6-b
2-i	7-h
3-a	8-e
4-j	9-f
5-g	10-c

The M.S. Level

1-g	6-i
2-f	7-e
3-j	8-d
4-a	9-h
5-c	10-b

The Ph.D. Level

1-b	6-g
2-c	7-e
3-f	8-a
4-i	9-h
5-j	10-d

Test 25:

The B.A. Level

1 Babe Ruth, Ted Williams
2 tackling
3 the side where the split end lines up
4 Jacques Plante
5 middleweight
6 126 pounds
7 Willie Mays
8 Joe DiMaggio
9 a strikeout
10 The Polo Grounds

The M.S. Level

1 the boundary lines on the long side of the field
2 Wes Unseld of the Baltimore Bullets
3 touching the ball during its downward arch toward the basket
4 a piece of turf knocked into the air when a golf club strikes the ground below the ball
5 Tom Seaver
6 welterweights
7 a fake punch used as a decoy
8 Philadelphia Warriors
9 the golfer with the best average in the PGA
10 102

The Ph.D. Level

1 $5\frac{1}{2}$–6 ounces
2 Boston Bruins
3 60 wins, 12 ties
4 Larry Csonka and Jim Kiick
5 Ernie Nevers of the Chicago Cardinals
6 Oklahoma
7 Nap Lajoie—.422 in 1901
8 sports editor Arch Ward of the *Chicago Tribune*
9 Jim Konstanty in 1950
10 one that covers a distance of less than a mile

Test 26:

The B.A. Level

1-f	7-l
2-j	8-c
3-g	9-h
4-a	10-e
5-k	11-i
6-b	12-d

The M.S. Level

1-c	7-f
2-d	8-k
3-a	9-b
4-h	10-g
5-l	11-i
6-j	12-e

The Ph.D. Level

1-k	7-l
2-f	8-c
3-i	9-d
4-h	10-e
5-a	11-g
6-j	12-b

Test 27:

The B.A. Level

1-j	6-b
2-g	7-f
3-e	8-d
4-i	9-c
5-a	10-h

The M.S. Level

1-f	6-h
2-g	7-a
3-e	8-d
4-i	9-b
5-j	10-c

The Ph.D. Level

1-d	6-c
2-i	7-e
3-a	8-f
4-g	9-j
5-b	10-h

Test 28:

The B.A. Level

1-g	6-i
2-e	7-a
3-h	8-b
4-d	9-f
5-j	10-c

The M.S. Level

1-g	6-a
2-d	7-i
3-h	8-c
4-j	9-e
5-b	10-f

The Ph.D. Level

1-i	6-c
2-a	7-b
3-h	8-f
4-g	9-e
5-j	10-d

Test 29:

The B.A. Level

1-h	6-i
2-d	7-f
3-a	8-c
4-j	9-g
5-b	10-e

The M.S. Level

1-b	6-i
2-g	7-h
3-a	8-f
4-e	9-c
5-j	10-d

The Ph.D. Level

1-i	6-c
2-a	7-e
3-j	8-g
4-b	9-f
5-h	10-d

Test 30:

The B.A. Level

1. Rochester, Minnesota
2. The Tower of London
3. Spain
4. Countess
5. Tin Lizzie
6. Tara
7. Admiral Robert E. Peary
8. Pygmalion
9. Alfred E. Neuman
10. Ron Turcotte

The M.S. Level

1. Leopold Bloom
2. Ed Gardner
3. Howard Barlow
4. Franklin D. Roosevelt
5. William Jennings Bryan
6. Britain and China
7. George Hartford
8. Freeman Gosden and Charles J. Correll
9. Augustus
10. none of them

The Ph.D. Level

1. Don Cornelius
2. the symbol of the medical profession
3. MacGuffin
4. Jan 1, 2001
5. Anne Hathaway
6. Roddy McDowall
7. France and Italy
8. Texas Guinan
9. The Nautilus
10. James Abbott McNeill Whistler

Test 31:

The B.A. Level

1-c	6-h
2-f	7-b
3-g	8-j
4-a	9-e
5-i	10-d

The M.S. Level

1-h	6-b
2-c	7-i
3-a	8-g
4-f	9-d
5-j	10-e

The Ph.D. Level

1-c	6-d
2-e	7-f
3-g	8-j
4-i	9-h
5-b	10-a

Test 32:

The B.A. Level

1-e	6-i
2-g	7-f
3-a	8-c
4-j	9-d
5-b	10-h

The M.S. Level

1-j	6-a
2-c	7-h
3-e	8-f
4-g	9-d
5-i	10-b

The Ph.D. Level

1-j	6-i
2-d	7-e
3-a	8-f
4-b	9-h
5-g	10-c

Test 33:

The B.A. Level

1-f	6-c
2-d	7-b
3-a	8-j
4-h	9-g
5-i	10-e

The M.S. Level

1-e	6-g
2-a	7-j
3-f	8-d
4-b	9-h
5-i	10-c

The Ph.D. Level

1-c	6-i
2-a	7-h
3-e	8-b
4-j	9-g
5-d	10-f

Test 34:

The B.A. Level

1-c	7-e
2-h	8-f
3-j	9-k
4-a	10-g
5-l	11-i
6-b	12-d

The M.S. Level

1-d	7-c
2-j	8-e
3-g	9-h
4-l	10-f
5-a	11-b
6-k	12-i

The Ph.D. Level

1-l	7-e
2-d	8-c
3-j	9-g
4-i	10-h
5-a	11-f
6-b	12-k

Test 35:

The B.A. Level

1 Tracy Lord
2 Fredric March
3 Oscar Levant
4 Love and Hate
5 Ygor
6 Betty Grable and June Haver
7 Jack Benny
8 Keye Luke
9 Peter Lorre
10 Edmond O'Brien

The M.S. Level

1 *My Darling Clementine*
2 Harry Carey
3 *Angels With Dirty Faces*
4 Judith Anderson
5 H. B. Warner
6 Roger Livesey
7 Joseph Tura
8 Dean Jagger and Helen Hayes
9 *I, Claudius*
10 Marlon Brando

The Ph.D. Level

1 Humphrey Bogart
2 Rex Ingram
3 Walter Huston and Rosemary de Camp
4 Julie Adams
5 *The Jungle Princess*
6 Mandrake Falls
7 Rondo Hatton
8 Jimmy Dodd, Bob Steele, Tom Tyler
9 Eduardo Ciannelli
10 Rudy Vallee

Test 36:

The B.A. Level

1 A; B; AB; O
2 Highest batting average; most home runs; most runs batted in
3 Smith; Johnson; Williams; Jones; Brown
4 James Caan and Billy Dee Williams
5 U.S. Grant; Rutherford B. Hayes; James A. Garfield; Benjamin Harrison; William McKinley; William Howard Taft; Warren G. Harding
6 Go; Free Parking; Go to Jail; Jail
7 Turkey Lurkey; Goosey Loosey; Ducky Lucky; Henny Penny; Chicken Little
8 Amy; Beth; Jo; Meg
9 Joseph Jr.; John; Rosemary; Kathleen; Eunice; Patricia; Robert; Jean; Edward
10 Steven Hill; Martin Landau; Barbara Bain; Peter Lupus; Greg Morris

The M.S. Level

1 Shadrach; Meshach; Abednego
2 Don Knotts; Louis Nye; Tom Poston; Bill Dana; Gabe Dell
3 Chemistry; Economics; Literature; Medicine/Physiology; Physics; Peace
4 thimble; iron; shoe; dog; battleship; top hat; cannon; race car
5 John Adams; John Quincy Adams; Theodore Roosevelt; Rutherford B. Hayes; Franklin D. Roosevelt; John F. Kennedy
6 Jets; Sharks
7 Mary Pickford; Douglas Fairbanks; D. W. Griffith; Charles Chaplin
8 *To Have and Have Not; Two Guys from Milwaukee; The Big Sleep; Dark Passage; Key Largo*
9 Goneril; Regan; Cordelia
10 Thelma Hopkins; Joyce Vincent Wilson

The Ph.D. Level

1 Atlanta, Ga.; Leavenworth, Kans.; Lewisburg, Pa.; McNeil Island, Wash.; Marion, Ill.; Terra Haute, Ind.
2 Cornelia; Pompera; Calpurnia
3 Deimos, Phobos
4 John Cassavetes; Charles Bronson; Jim Brown; Telly Savalas; Donald Sutherland; Clint Walker; Trini Lopez; Tom Busby; Ben Carruthers; Stuart Cooper; Colin Maitland; Al Mancini
5 *Come and Get It; Kentucky; The Westerner*
6 grammar; logic; rhetoric; arithmetic; geometry; astronomy; music
7 incisors; cuspids; bicuspids; molars
8 Brahma; Shiva; Vishnu
9 Aurora Australis; Aurora Borealis
10 Yum-Yum; Beep-Bo; Pitti-Sing

Test 37:

The B.A. Level

1-i	6-g
2-c	7-d
3-f	8-e
4-a	9-h
5-j	10-b

The M.S. Level

1-h	6-d
2-i	7-f
3-j	8-e
4-a	9-g
5-c	10-b

The Ph.D. Level

1-f	6-c
2-e	7-d
3-i	8-h
4-b	9-j
5-g	10-a

Test 38:

The B.A. Level

1-c	6-i
2-g	7-e
3-d	8-j
4-h	9-a
5-f	10-b

The M.S. Level

1-i	6-h
2-f	7-e
3-b	8-a
4-j	9-d
5-g	10-c

The Ph.D. Level

1-d	6-b
2-a	7-j
3-f	8-c
4-i	9-h
5-g	10-e

Test 39:

The B.A. Level

1-c	6-d
2-g	7-e
3-j	8-f
4-a	9-b
5-i	10-h

The M.S. Level

1-g	6-e
2-c	7-d
3-i	8-b
4-a	9-h
5-j	10-f

The Ph.D. Level

1-c	6-i
2-f	7-e
3-a	8-j
4-g	9-h
5-b	10-d

Test 40:

The B.A. Level

1 Oakland Raiders
2 none, it is an independent
3 five yards
4 Yale
5 Chicago Black Hawks
6 30 feet
7 one, to Harry Greb
8 Joe B. Hall
9 Gaylord Perry
10 Lou Gehrig—2130

The M.S. Level

1 gold—javelin, silver—high-jump
2 3 times—1932, 1960, 1980
3 Gale Sayers
4 Boston Patriots
5 Notre Dame
6 chin; temples; stomach
7 knockout; technical knockout; decision
8 1938
9 Philadelphia 76ers
10 Yogi Berra—10

The Ph.D. Level

1 Lou Gehrig, Mickey Mantle
2 Orven Wilson in 1912
3 Honus Wagner
4 141
5 Primo Carnera
6 Denver Nuggets; New York Nets; San Antonio Spurs; Indiana Pacers
7 1947
8 The Royal Montreal Golf Club
9 Yelbeston Abraham
10 Jets 16, Colts 7

Test 41:

The B.A. Level

1-e	6-j
2-d	7-b
3-h	8-f
4-i	9-g
5-a	10-c

The M.S. Level

1-h	6-d
2-j	7-c
3-a	8-f
4-b	9-e
5-i	10-g

The Ph.D. Level

1-b	6-i
2-d	7-c
3-g	8-f
4-a	9-e
5-h	10-j

Test 42:

The B.A. Level

1-f	7-d
2-j	8-k
3-l	9-e
4-a	10-b
5-c	11-h
6-i	12-g

The M.S. Level

1-k	7-d
2-g	8-a
3-f	9-e
4-j	10-b
5-c	11-i
6-l	12-h

The Ph.D. Level

1-d	7-k
2-i	8-l
3-j	9-g
4-c	10-f
5-b	11-e
6-a	12-h

Test 43:

The B.A. Level

1-f	6-d
2-i	7-c
3-a	8-j
4-b	9-g
5-h	10-e

The M.S. Level

1-i	6-h
2-e	7-c
3-j	8-d
4-a	9-g
5-b	10-f

The Ph.D. Level

1-b	6-i
2-j	7-d
3-e	8-f
4-h	9-g
5-a	10-c

Test 44:

The B.A. Level

1-g	6-e
2-h	7-j
3-a	8-f
4-i	9-c
5-d	10-b

The M.S. Level

1-g	6-j-b
2-a	7-h
3-c	8-f
4-e	9-b
5-i	10-d

The Ph.D. Level

1-b	6-j
2-c	7-d
3-f	8-h
4-g	9-e
5-a	10-i

Test 45:

The B.A. Level

1. *Semper Fidelis*
2. Good to the Last Drop
3. Klingons
4. Handsome Dan
5. U.S.S.R.; China; Canada
6. *Divine Comedy,* by Dante
7. *The Sun Also Rises*
8. Booker T. Washington
9. Newport, R.I.
10. *The Great Train Robbery*

The M.S. Level

1. St. Helena
2. Rodney
3. William McKinley
4. Ovaltine
5. "The best is yet to be"
6. source of mystery
7. *Tea and Sympathy*
8. *The Merry Wives of Windsor*
9. "A stately pleasure-dome decree"
10. Howard da Silva

The Ph.D. Level

1. San Simeon, California
2. The 7–10 split in bowling
3. Schuyler
4. bookish and pedantic
5. The Louvre
6. The Lord Be with You
7. Walter Scott
8. Hegira
9. The Angel Waterfall in Venezuela—3,281 ft. high
10. *The Mystery of Edwin Drood*

Test 46:

The B.A. Level

1-e	7-b
2-j	8-k
3-a	9-f
4-h	10-g
5-c	11-i
6-l	12-d

The M.S. Level

1-j	7-f
2-d	8-b
3-h	9-k
4-a	10-i
5-l	11-g
6-e	12-c

The Ph.D. Level

1-e	7-k
2-j	8-i
3-g	9-d
4-a	10-b
5-l	11-h
6-c	12-f

Test 47:

The B.A. Level

1-d	7-c
2-g	8-e
3-k	9-f
4-l	10-h
5-i	11-b
6-a	12-j

The M.S. Level

1-d	7-k
2-h	8-b
3-g	9-c
4-f	10-l
5-a	11-e
6-j	12-i

The Ph.D. Level

1-f	7-c
2-g	8-b
3-e	9-k
4-a	10-i
5-d	11-l
6-h	12-j

Test 48:

The B.A. Level

1-c	6-a
2-d	7-j
3-g	8-e
4-f	9-b
5-i	10-h

The M.S. Level

1-h	6-c
2-a	7-j
3-g	8-d
4-b	9-e
5-i	10-f

The Ph.D. Level

1-b	6-i
2-e	7-j
3-f	8-g
4-h	9-c
5-d	10-a

Test 49:

The B.A. Level

1-j	7-d
2-f	8-l
3-a	9-e
4-h	10-g
5-b	11-k
6-i	12-c

The M.S. Level

1-d	7-i
2-c	8-b
3-f	9-e
4-a	10-h
5-k	11-g
6-l	12-j

The Ph.D. Level

1-i	7-j
2-g	8-a
3-l	9-f
4-d	10-e
5-b	11-h
6-k	12-c

Test 50:

The B.A. Level

1 Walter Huston
2 Freddie Bartholemew
3 Woody Strode
4 *PT-109*
5 Bert Lahr
6 Rome
7 Gary Cooper
8 Hermione Gingold
9 Charles Laughton
10 Ingrid Bergman

The M.S. Level

1 Edward Arnold
2 George Burns
3 Simone Simon
4 Gale Sondergaard
5 John Mills
6 Teresa Wright
7 Shirley Temple
8 an antique car
9 Mercedes McCambridge
10 *Royal Wedding*

The Ph.D. Level

1 Laird Cregar
2 both played Judge Roy Bean
3 Bing Crosby
4 *The Seventh Seal*
5 George Tobias
6 *The Paper Chase*
7 *The Bachelor and the Bobby-Soxer*
8 *Notorious*
9 Miklos Rozsa
10 Emmett Kelly

Test 51:

The B.A. Level

1 Animal; Vegetable; Mineral
2 Norway; Sweden; Denmark; Iceland; Finland
3 Karen; Richard
4 South Carolina; Mississippi; Florida; Alabama; Georgia; Louisiana; Texas; Virginia; Tennessee; Arkansas; North Carolina
5 Wyatt; Virgil; Morgan
6 Bingo, a gorilla; Drooper, a lion; Fleagle, a dog; Snarky, a baby elephant
7 yellow; red; orange; green; white
8 fire; earth; water; air
9 Dianne; Peggy; Janet; Kathy
10 Brian Wilson; Carl Wilson; Al Jardine; Bruce Johnston; Mike Love; Dennis Wilson

The M.S. Level

1 New South Wales; Queensland; South Australia; Tasmania; Victoria; Western Australia; Northern Territory
2 *Mutiny on the Bounty; Men Against the Sea; Pitcairn's Island*
3 Delaware; Pennsylvania; New Jersey; Georgia; Connecticut; Massachusetts; Maryland; South Carolina; New Hampshire; Virginia; New York; North Carolina; Rhode Island
4 Horace; John
5 knife; revolver; wrench; lead pipe; rope; candlestick
6 Kenesaw "Mountain" Landis; Albert "Happy" Chandler; Ford Frick; William Eckart; Bowie Kuhn
7 Kid Shelleen; Tim Strawn
8 California; Florida; Texas
9 Don; Phil
10 U.S.; U.S.S.R.; United Kingdom; France; China

The Ph.D. Level

1 Virgil "Gus" Grissom; Edward White; Roger Chaffee
2 Cherokees; Choctaws, Chickasaws; Creeks; Seminoles
3 Ham; Shem; Japheth
4 bury the dead; clothe the naked; feed the hungry; give drink to the thirsty; house the homeless; tend the sick; visit the fatherless and afflicted
5 Ed; Gene; Joe; Vic
6 Anastasia; Drizella
7 Yugoslavia; Albania; Greece; Romania; Bulgaria; European Turkey
8 Genesis; Exodus; Leviticus; Numbers; Deuteronomy
9 Donald Pleasance; Telly Savalas; Charles Gray
10 tiger; hare; dragon; snake; horse; sheep; monkey; rooster; dog; pig; rat; ox

Test 52:

The B.A. Level

1-g	6-b
2-j	7-f
3-d	8-a
4-c	9-e
5-h	10-i

The M.S. Level

1-j	6-g
2-d	7-c
3-i	8-b
4-e	9-f
5-a	10-h

The Ph.D. Level

1-d	6-c
2-j	7-i
3-h	8-g
4-a	9-f
5-b	10-e

Test 53:

The B.A. Level

1-i	6-h
2-f	7-c
3-e	8-j
4-g	9-b
5-d	10-a

The M.S. Level

1-j	6-a
2-g	7-c
3-i	8-d
4-b	9-f
5-e	10-h

The Ph.D. Level

1-b	6-f
2-i	7-e
3-j	8-d
4-a	9-g
5-h	10-c

Test 54:

The B.A. Level

1-e	7-l
2-h	8-c
3-a	9-f
4-i	10-d
5-k	11-j
6-b	12-g

The M.S. Level

1-g	7-b
2-k	8-d
3-e	9-c
4-l	10-j
5-a	11-h
6-i	12-f

The Ph.D. Level

1-i	7-l
2-k	8-j
3-e	9-d
4-g	10-f
5-a	11-c
6-b	12-h

Test 55:

The B.A. Level

1-d	6-e
2-i	7-j-d
3-g	8-b
4-a	9-h
5-c	10-f

The M.S. Level

1-f	6-j
2-a	7-h
3-b	8-e
4-g	9-d
5-i	10-c

The Ph.D. Level

1-d	6-j
2-f	7-c
3-a	8-g
4-b	9-e
5-h	10-i

Test 56:

The B.A. Level

1-b	6-d
2-b	7-c
3-b	8-b
4-c	9-a
5-c	10-c

The M.S. Level

1-b	6-a
2-d	7-a
3-c	8-b
4-b	9-d
5-b	10-b

The Ph.D. Level

1-b	6-c
2-b	7-d
3-a	8-a
4-b	9-d
5-d	10-a

Test 57:

The B.A. Level

1-g	6-c
2-j	7-f
3-h	8-i
4-a	9-e
5-b	10-d

The M.S. Level

1-i	6-g
2-d	7-f
3-e	8-a
4-h	9-c
5-j	10-b

The Ph.D. Level

1-c	6-b
2-f	7-i
3-a	8-e
4-h	9-g
5-j	10-d

Test 58:

The B.A. Level

1-b	6-a
2-d	7-c
3-a	8-c
4-b	9-b
5-a	10-d

The M.S. Level

1-c	6-d
2-b	7-a
3-c	8-a
4-a	9-d
5-b	10-c

The Ph.D. Level

1-a	6-b
2-d	7-b
3-c	8-c
4-a	9-d
5-c	10-a

Test 59:

The B.A. Level

1 eat fat
2 fetching a pail of water
3 Banbury Cross
4 the farmer's wife
5 her lamb
6 the dish
7 three bags full
8 a pig
9 four and twenty
10 he ran away

The M.S. Level

1 a penny
2 his pipe, his bowl, his fiddlers three
3 butcher, baker, candlestick maker
4 Humpty Dumpty
5 a rabbit skin
6 a crooked sixpence
7 yellow
8 under a haystack, fast asleep
9 gate
10 in the pot, nine days old

The Ph.D. Level

1 Tommy Stout
2 his night gown
3 Sukey
4 in his mother's pail
5 dead
6 white bread and butter
7 Drury Lane
8 a Christmas pie
9 cold and frosty
10 among the cinders

Test 60:

The B.A. Level

1 George Jessel
2 Willie Loman
3 "Dominique"
4 Dr. Steven Kiley
5 "Sweet Georgia Brown"
6 Robert Frost
7 Holden Caulfield
8 Charles Goodyear
9 Theodore Roosevelt
10 daydreamer

The M.S. Level

1 Lloyd C. Douglas
2 the communist equivalent of NATO
3 the Dead Sea Scrolls
4 Walter Winchell
5 Laika
6 Plaza de Major
7 provenance
8 Algy
9 Hollywood Argyles
10 Sparkle

The Ph.D. Level

1 H.M.S. Resolution
2 Penelope
3 Felicia Sanders
4 one who collects picture postcards
5 Edward Gaedel
6 amyotrophic lateral sclerosis
7 Industrial Workers of the World
8 Washington, D.C.
9 by the lines on the palm of the hand
10 Lippizan

Test 61:

The B.A. Level

1-h	7-d
2-k	8-e
3-a	9-f
4-l	10-g
5-b	11-j
6-i	12-c

The M.S. Level

1-f	7-c
2-j	8-k
3-b	9-e
4-g	10-h
5-a	11-i
6-l	12-d

The Ph.D. Level

1-j	7-l
2-f	8-d
3-g	9-e
4-i	10-c
5-a	11-h
6-b	12-k

Test 62:

The B.A. Level

1-c	6-b
2-g	7-e
3-j	8-f
4-a	9-h
5-i	10-d

The M.S. Level

1-d	6-c
2-a	7-f
3-i	8-j
4-g	9-b
5-h	10-e

The Ph.D. Level

1-f	6-i
2-d	7-e
3-a	8-j
4-h	9-g
5-c	10-b

Test 63:

The B.A. Level

1-e	7-j
2-g	8-f
3-l	9-a
4-k	10-d
5-c	11-b
6-i	12-h

The M.S. Level

1-f	7-k
2-g	8-i
3-j	9-e
4-l	10-h
5-b	11-d
6-c	12-a

The Ph.D. Level

1-h	7-d
2-i	8-k
3-g	9-j
4-b	10-e
5-l	11-c
6-a	12-f

Test 64:

The B.A. Level

1 Katharine Hepburn
2 James Cagney
3 Peter Sellers
4 Ann-Margret
5 Ursula Andress
6 Marlon Brando
7 Edward G. Robinson
8 Don Murray
9 Clint Eastwood
10 Susan Hayward

The M.S. Level

1 Paul Newman
2 Ryan O'Neal
3 Spencer Tracy
4 Shelley Winters
5 Eleanor Parker
6 Julie Andrews
7 June Allyson
8 Walter Matthau
9 Jack Lemmon
10 Janet Leigh

The Ph.D. Level

1 Dick Van Dyke
2 Walter Huston
3 Judy Holliday
4 Rhonda Fleming
5 Lauren Bacall
6 Warren Beatty
7 Tallulah Bankhead
8 Ralph Bellamy
9 Rock Hudson
10 Jean Simmons

Test 65:

The B.A. Level

1 Irene Ryan
2 Jackie Gleason
3 Tommy Smothers to Dickie
4 Judy Carne
5 Jonathan Winters
6 Cliff Arquette
7 LeVar Burton
8 *All In The Family*
9 Phyllis Lindstrom
10 ABC's *Wide World of Sports*
11 Shirley Booth
12 Bob and Ray

The M.S. Level

1 Ted Bessell
2 Agnes Moorehead
3 Gale Gordon
4 Maynard G. Krebs
5 Six
6 Fred
7 Loretta Haggers
8 *The Flintstones*
9 Alistair Cooke
10 Joe E. Ross
11 George Takei
12 Paul Drake on *Perry Mason*

The Ph.D. Level

1 Jolene Brand
2 Julie Newmar
3 Miss Sookie
4 Alan Napier
5 Allison Mackenzie, Rodney Harrington
6 John Drake
7 *Beacon Hill*
8 Judd Hirsch
9 Tim Considine
10 Douglas Edwards
11 Marion Lorne; Durwood Kirby; Carol Burnett
12 Katharine Hepburn; Laurence Olivier

Test 66:

The B.A. Level

1-d	6-g
2-j	7-e
3-a	8-c
4-i	9-h
5-f	10-b

The M.S. Level

1-g	6-i
2-j	7-h
3-b	8-d
4-a	9-e
5-c	10-f

The Ph.D. Level

1-b	6-i
2-f	7-d
3-h	8-e
4-g	9-j
5-a	10-c

Test 67:

The B.A. Level

1 Dick Van Dyke; Morey Amsterdam; Rose Marie
2 hearts; moons; stars; clovers; diamonds
3 Aries, the ram; Taurus, the bull; Gemini, the twins; Cancer, the crab; Leo, the lion; Virgo, the virgin; Libra, the balance; Scorpio, the scorpion; Sagittarius, the archer; Capricorn, the goat; Aquarius, the water carrier; Pisces, the fish
4 Pat O'Brien; Walter Brennan; Edgar Buchanan
5 April; May; June
6 meter; liter; gram
7 parallelograms; rhombi; rectangles; squares; trapezoids
8 Delaware; North Carolina; South Carolina; Pennsylvania
9 China; India; U.S.S.R.; U.S.A.
10 Vincent; Joseph; Domenic

The M.S. Level

1 Stheno; Euryale; Medusa
2 1-yellow; 2-blue; 3-red; 4-purple; 5-orange; 6-green; 7-plum; 8-black; cueball-white
3 Beaver—Jerry Mathers; Wally—Tony Dow; father—Hugh Beaumont; mother—Barbara Billingsley

4 Gaston; Louis
5 *Woman of the Year; Keeper of the Flame; Without Love; The Sea of Grass; State of the Union; Adam's Rib; Pat and Mike; The Desk Set; Guess Who's Coming to Dinner?*
6 *The Bastard; The Rebels; The Seekers; The Furies; The Titans; The Warriors*
7 Perry Mason; Della Street; Hamilton Burger; Lt. Arthur Tragg; Paul Drake
8 Sarek and Amanda
9 water turned to blood; frogs; lice; flies; cattle murdered; sores; hail and fire; locusts; darkness; slaying of Egyptian firstborn

The Ph.D. Level

1 Mrs. Mary Surratt; Donald Herold; Lewis Paine; George Atzerodt
2 trustworthy, loyal, helpful, friendly, courteous, kind, obedient, cheerful, thrifty, brave, clean, reverent
3 Eddie Cicotte—P; Happy Felsch—CF; Chick Gaudil—1st; Joe Jackson—RF; Fred McMullen—UIF; Swede Risberg—SS; Buck Weaver—3rd; Claude Williams—P
4 Jacob Ludwig; Wilhelm Karl
5 Babe Ruth; Lou Gehrig; Jimmy Foxx; Al Simmons; Joe Cronin
6 Chester; Albert; Barney; Walter
7 tetrahedron; cube; octahedron; dodecahedron; icosahedron
8 Molly; Jake; Uncle David; Rosalie; Sammy
9 Ernie Hare; Billy Jones
10 Clifton Fadiman; John Kieran; Franklin Pierce Adams

Test 68:

The B.A. Level

1-h	7-d
2-e	8-f
3-i	9-l
4-a	10-g
5-k	11-j
6-c	12-b

The M.S. Level

1-e	7-c
2-i	8-l
3-g	9-f
4-k	10-a
5-h	11-b
6-d	12-j

The Ph.D. Level

1-c	7-b
2-g	8-a
3-i	9-l
4-j	10-k
5-h	11-e
6-d	12-f

Test 69:

The B.A. Level

1-e,j
2-m,p
3-a,q
4-h,k
5-i,o
6-b,g
7-c,s
8-l,n
9-d,r
10-f,t

The M.S. Level

1-g,l
2-i,p
3-e,t
4-a,f
5-o,r
6-m,s
7-c,h
8-n,q
9-d,k
10-b,j

The Ph.D. Level

1-f,i
2-d,o
3-a,j
4-h,s
5-k,l
6-m,r
7-c,q
8-g,n
9-p,t
10-b,e

Test 70:

The B.A. Level

1 Emerald City
2 Fala
3 Flower
4 *Chicago Tribune*
5 Toby
6 intercontinental missile
7 *Mona Lisa*
8 Office of Public Administration
9 Mayor Fiorello LaGuardia
10 Goliath

The M.S. Level

1 Tabitha
2 William Wambsganss
3 Ural
4 Snively Whiplash
5 the Sparrow
6 *Twixt Twelve and Twenty*
7 bad money will drive good money out of circulation
8 Leper Colony
9 Trygve Lie of Norway
10 Chase and Sanborn coffee

The Ph.D. Level

1 Grover Cleveland
2 Vincent Furnier
3 "I Can't Give You Anything but Love, Baby"
4 A & W root beer stands (1922)
5 "Pitching Horseshoes"
6 Bobby Franks
7 "The Parliament of Fools"
8 DeWitt Wallace
9 Uncas
10 −273.16°C, which equals −459.69°F

Test 71:

The B.A. Level

1 John and Ethel Barrymore
2 Ingmar and Ingrid Bergman
3 Adam and Mae West
4 Lynn and Vanessa Redgrave
5 Audie and George Murphy
6 Margaret and Pat O'Brien
7 Jane and Rosalind Russell
8 Alan and Robert Alda
9 Broderick and Joan Crawford
10 Deborah and John Kerr

The M.S. Level

1 Janet and Vivien Leigh
2 Gene and Grace Kelly
3 Connie and Craig Stevens
4 John and Maureen O'Hara
5 Gracie and Steve Allen
6 Lee and Susan Strasberg
7 Butterfly and Steve McQueen
8 Dean and Jennifer Jones
9 Liza and Vincente Minnelli
10 Jay and Sheree North

The Ph.D. Level

1 Dina and Gary Merrill
2 Frank and Helen Morgan
3 Robert and Roland Young
4 Christopher and Gypsy Rose Lee
5 Bruce and Joan Bennett
6 David and H. B. Warner
7 Jesse and Pearl White
8 Elaine and James Stewart
9 Charles "Buddy" and Ginger Rogers
10 Donald and Una O'Connor

Test 72:

The B.A. Level

1-f 6-i
2-a 8-e
3-j 8-h
4-g 9-d
5-b 10-c

The M.S. Level

1-c 6-e
2-h 7-d
3-i 8-f
4-a 9-g
5-j 10-b

The Ph.D. Level

1-e 6-h
2-g 7-b
3-a 8-i
4-j 9-c
5-d 10-f

Test 73:

The B.A. Level

1-f 7-c
2-i 8-g
3-e 9-h
4-a 10-b
5-l 11-d
6-k 12-j

The M.S. Level

1-j 7-a
2-g 8-f
3-e 9-h
4-k 10-d
5-b 11-c
6-l 12-i

The Ph.D. Level

1-g 7-e
2-l 8-b
3-h 9-k
4-j 10-d
5-a 11-f
6-i 12-c

Test 74:

The B.A. Level

1-d	7-i
2-h	8-b
3-j	9-l
4-f	10-e
5-k	11-c
6-a	12-g

The M.S. Level

1-d	7-k
2-j	8-a
3-e	9-l
4-g	10-i
5-c	11-f
6-h	12-b

The Ph.D. Level

1-b	7-e
2-h	8-l
3-f	9-g
4-j	10-a
5-c	11-i
6-d	12-k

Test 75:

The B.A. Level

1-f	6-c
2-a	7-e
3-i	8-h
4-b	9-g
5-j	10-d

The M.S. Level

1-g	6-i
2-d	7-h
3-a	8-e
4-j	9-f
5-b	10-c

The Ph.D. Level

1-i	6-f
2-e	7-h
3-a	8-g
4-j	9-d
5-c	10-b

Test 76:

The B.A. Level

1-f	6-g
2-h	7-j
3-a	8-c
4-i	9-d
5-b	10-e

The M.S. Level

1-g	6-d
2-c	7-b
3-a	8-e
4-i	9-f
5-j	10-h

The Ph.D. Level

1-j	6-h
2-d	7-i
3-a	8-e
4-b	9-f
5-g	10-c

Test 77:

The B.A. Level

1-e	6-j
2-d	7-c
3-b	8-f
4-a	9-h
5-g	10-i

The M.S. Level

1-i	6-c
2-j	7-d
3-e	8-f
4-a	9-b
5-g	10-h

The Ph.D. Level

1-c	6-j
2-d	7-e
3-h	8-f
4-g	9-i
5-b	10-a

Test 78:

The B.A. Level

1 Lilli and Peter Palmer
2 Burt and Debbie Reynolds
3 Donna and Oliver Reed
4 Eleanor and Fess Parker
5 Joseph and Raquel Welch
6 Elizabeth and Robert Taylor
7 Clifton and Jack Webb
8 Alan and Loretta Young
9 Esther and Guy Williams
10 Patty and Myron McCormack

The M.S. Level

1 Arthur and Veronica Lake
2 Dean and Mary Martin
3 Edie and Nick Adams
4 Eddie "Rochester" and Dame Judith Anderson
5 Dana and Julie Andrews
6 Ed and Keenan Wynn
7 Cornel and Oscar Wilde
8 Forest and Sophie Tucker
9 Gene and June Lockhart
10 Carroll and Stanley Baker

The Ph.D. Level

1 Leo G. and Madeleine Carroll
2 George S. and Christine Kaufman
3 Natalie and Sam Wood
4 Peggy and Robert Ryan
5 George and Sylvia Sidney
6 Grace and Victor Moore
7 Barbara and Mike Nichols
8 Joan and Ray Collins
9 Gene and Lawrence Tierney
10 Alexis and C. Aubrey Smith

Test 79:

The B.A. Level

1-h	7-j
2-e	8-d
3-k	9-c
4-a	10-g
5-l	11-i
6-b	12-f

The M.S. Level

1-j	7-d
2-g	8-c
3-i	9-f
4-l	10-k
5-h	11-e
6-a	12-b

The Ph.D. Level

1-d	7-k
2-h	8-e
3-a	9-l
4-f	10-c
5-b	11-j
6-i	12-g

Test 80:

The B.A. Level

1 Give Service
2 Jack
3 William and Mary College
4 Eddie Arcaro
5 Gov
6 Anatevka
7 *Rasputin and the Empress*
8 Combination of Jack of Diamonds and Queen of Spades
9 Fernwood, Ohio
10 he wanted to expiate an act of cowardice

The M.S. Level

1 the earliest known form of a word
2 very dry, shaken rather than stirred
3 Thomas Cup
4 *Somebody Up There Likes Me*
5 Edgar Allan Poe
6 Carol Burnett
7 *Liberty*
8 In a hierarchy, every employee tends to rise to his level of incompetence
9 Kelso
10 dictionary

The Ph.D. Level

1 a pause in a line or at the end of a poem
2 calm, peaceful, untroubled by care or worry
3 Major Henry Wirz, commandant of the Confederate military prison Andersonville
4 Ahdet Bey
5 a Pooka
6 "After all, tomorrow is another day."
7 Jane Austen
8 Stephen Vincent Benét's *The Devil and Daniel Webster*
9 Justerini and Brooks
10 Jackson, Miss.; Jefferson City, Missouri; Madison, Wisc.; Lincoln, Nebraska

Test 81

The B.A. Level

1-d	6-a
2-f	7-j
3-f	8-e
4-b	9-h
5-g	10-c

The M.S. Level

1-i	6-d
2-e	7-c
3-a	8-j
4-h	9-f
5-b	10-g

The Ph.D. Level

1-b	6-g
2-a	7-f
3-h	8-j
4-i	9-e
5-c	10-d

Test 82:

The B.A. Level

1-f,k	6-d,m
2-i,n	7-e,j
3-g,r	8-c,h
4-b,o	9-q,s
5-l,t	10-a,p

The M.S. Level

1-e,h	6-b,i
2-f,m	7-j,n
3-p,s	8-o,r
4-a,l	9-c,t
5-k,q	10-d,g

The Ph.D. Level

1-e,g	6-c,s
2-k,m	7-h,q
3-f,j	8-o,p
4-a,i	9-l,t
5-n,r	10-b,d

Test 83:

The B.A. Level		The M.S. Level		The Ph.D. Level	
1-f	6-i	1-i	6-h	1-f	6-j
2-j	7-c	2-f	7-b	2-a	7-e
3-a	8-e	3-j	8-e	3-g	8-c
4-h	9-g	4-a	9-d	4-h	9-d
5-b	10-d	5-c	10-g	5-b	10-i

Test 84:

The B.A. Level		The M.S. Level		The Ph.D. Level	
1-h	6-c	1-e	6-g	1-d	6-b
2-d	7-j	2-h	7-j	2-a	7-i
3-g	8-e	3-a	8-f	3-h	8-c
4-a	9-f	4-i	9-c	4-f	9-g
5-i	10-b	5-d	10-b	5-e	10-j

Test 85:

The B.A. Level		The M.S. Level		The Ph.D. Level	
1-f-III	6-i-X	1-e-III	6-c-I	1-e-IV	6-b-VI
2-j-VI	7-d-II	2-j-VI	7-d-X	2-c-V	7-i-I
3-a-VIII	8-e-IX	3-g-V	8-f-IX	3-h-X	8-f-IX
4-b-V	9-g-IV	4-a-II	9-h-IV	4-a-III	9-g-II
5-h-I	10-c-VII	5-i-VIII	10-b-VII	5-j-VIII	10-d-VII

Test 86:

The B.A. Level		The M.S. Level		The Ph.D. Level	
1-e	6-a	1-i	6-h	1-d	6-j
2-h	7-i	2-g	7-d	2-f	7-g
3-f	8-g	3-e	8-f	3-a	8-e
4-b	9-d	4-j	9-b	4-h	9-b
5-j	10-c	5-c	10-a	5-c	10-i

Test 87:

The B.A. Level		The M.S. Level		The Ph.D. Level	
1-f	6-d	1-f	6-j	1-c	6-i
2-i	7-g	2-d	7-e	2-f	7-j
3-h	8-c	3-i	8-c	3-h	8-e
4-b	9-e	4-h	9-g	4-b	9-g
5-j	10-a	5-b	10-a	5-a	10-d

Test 88:

The B.A. Level

1 *Summer of '42*
2 *To Catch a Thief*
3 *Who's Afraid of Virginia Woolf?*
4 *The Goodbye Girl*
5 *The Candidate*
6 *Never on Sunday*
7 *In the Heat of the Night*
8 *Klute*
9 *Cat Ballou*
10 *Picnic*
11 *The Third Man*
12 *Harry and Tonto*

The M.S. Level

1 *The Heiress*
2 *Butterflies Are Free*
3 *Johnny Belinda*
4 *Ryan's Daughter*
5 *The Lost Weekend*
6 *Whatever Happened to Baby Jane?*
7 *A Tree Grows in Brooklyn*
8 *Separate Tables*
9 *The Solid Gold Cadillac*
10 *Alice Doesn't Live Here Any More*
11 *Portrait of Jennie*
12 *The Good Earth*

The Ph.D. Level

1 *Love Me or Leave Me*
2 *The Razor's Edge*
3 *Kitty Foyle*
4 *The Barefoot Contessa*
5 *It Happened One Night*
6 *A Touch of Class*
7 *A Hole in the Head*
8 *Sabrina*
9 *Spellbound*
10 *Panic in the Streets*
11 *The Rose Tattoo*
12 *Suspicion*

Test 89:

The B.A. Level

1-f	6-h
2-i	7-j
3-a	8-e
4-c	9-d
5-b	10-g

The M.S. Level

1-c	6-d
2-e	7-f
3-g	8-j
4-i	9-h
5-a	10-b

The Ph.D. Level

1-e	6-c
2-a	7-j
3-f	8-i
4-b	8-d
5-g	10-h

Test 90:

The B.A. Level

1 Josephine
2 goat
3 *Romeo and Juliet*
4 fell on his sword
5 Wheaties
6 Arizona—1912
7 Charles Lutwidge Dodgson
8 Aunt Em
9 Atlantic City, New Jersey
10 root beer

The M.S. Level

1 Rumpelstiltskin
2 St. George
3 Sam Catchem
4 Do a Good Turn Daily
5 Seth
6 Moon Maids
7 Mt. Sinai
8 Excalibur
9 Ron Galella
10 Robert Frost

The Ph.D. Level

1 *The Great Gatsby*
2 *Justine; Balthazar; Mountolive; Clea*
3 T. S. Eliot in "The Hollow Men"
4 Clara Patacci
5 *The American Mercury*
6 Packard automobiles
7 the Statue of Liberty
8 Singapore
9 a verse or sentence which is the same when read either forward or backward
10 New Orleans

Test 91:

The B.A. Level

1-b	6-c
2-a	7-c
3-d	8-d
4-b	9-c
5-a	10-b

The M.S. Level

1-a	6-a
2-d	7-c
3-b	8-b
4-b	9-a
5-a	10-d

The Ph.D. Level

1-d	6-a
2-b	7-d
3-a	8-d
4-c	9-a
5-b	10-b

Test 92:

The B.A. Level

1-d	7-e
2-h	8-l
3-i	9-g
4-a	10-f
5-c	11-j
6-k	12-b

The M.S. Level

1-h	7-k
2-l	8-f
3-a	9-e
4-i	10-g
5-c	11-b
6-d	12-j

The Ph.D. Level

1-k	7-l
2-f	8-e
3-g	9-a
4-b	10-h
5-i	11-c
6-d	12-j

Test 93:

The B.A. Level

1-c-i	6-g
2-f	7-i
3-a	8-d
4-h	9-e
5-j	10-b

The M.S. Level

1-c-i	6-h
2-i	7-b-h
3-a	8-f
4-j	9-e
5-d	10-g

The Ph.D. Level

1-f	6-c
2-d	7-j
3-h	8-e
4-a	9-b
5-i	10-g

Test 94:

The B.A. Level

1-h	7-c
2-e	8-l
3-j	9-b
4-a	10-i
5-k	11-g
6-d	12-f

The M.S. Level

1-d	7-l
2-a	8-k
3-g	9-f
4-i	10-h
5-j	11-e
6-c	12-b

The Ph.D. Level

1-e	7-a
2-d	8-f
3-h	9-j
4-k	10-c
5-l	11-g
6-b	12-i

Test 95:

The B.A. Level

1-i-VI	6-h-V
2-f-VII	7-b-I
3-g-IX	8-e-VIII
4-j-III	9-a-IV
5-d-II	10-c-X

The M.S. Level

1-i-V	6-h-II
2-a-IX	7-j-III
3-e-VI	8-g-VIII
4-c-I	9-f-VII
5-d-X	10-b-IV

The Ph.D. Level

1-g-IV	6-e-V
2-c-VIII	7-d-IX
3-h-III	8-j-II
4-a-VII	9-f-VI
5-i-I	10-b-X

Test 96:

The B.A. Level

1-b	7-d
2-g	8-e
3-i	9-f
4-j	10-a
5-k	11-h
6-l	12-c

The M.S. Level

1-g	7-d
2-h	8-a
3-j	9-f
4-l	10-c
5-i	11-e
6-k	12-b

The Ph.D. Level

1-i	7-b
2-e	8-k
3-l	9-f
4-a	10-c
5-h	11-g
6-j	12-d

Test 97:

The B.A. Level

1-g	6-d
2-i	7-b
3-e	8-f
4-a	9-c
5-j	10-h

The M.S. Level

1-i	6-a
2-c	7-e
3-f	8-d
4-b	9-h
5-j	10-g

The Ph.D. Level

1-c	6-b
2-d	7-e
3-f	8-a
4-h	9-j
5-i	10-g

Test 98:

The B.A. Level

1-f	6-i
2-c	7-d
3-h	8-g
4-b	9-a
5-j	10-e

The M.S. Level

1-f	6-a
2-c	7-i
3-h	8-e
4-j	9-d
5-g	10-b

The Ph.D. Level

1-d	6-i
2-e	7-c
3-g	8-j
4-a	9-h
5-f	10-b

Test 99:

The B.A. Level

1. *A Glass Menagerie*
2. Plato
3. Ben Franklin and a mouse
4. Manners
5. Woodrow Wilson
6. The Spaniards
7. Judge Weaver
8. a red *A* embroidered on Hester Prynne's dress, meaning "adulteress"
9. St. Patrick
10. Alan Alda

The M.S. Level

1. Ernestine
2. Yale University
3. *Adventure*
4. Gaylord
5. H.M.S. *Beagle*
6. Chuck Parker
7. the Erie Canal
8. Colonel Owen Thursday
9. Digger O'Dell
10. Mary Baker Eddy

The Ph.D. Level

1. Jimmy Stewart
2. *Romola*
3. *Shamrock*
4. strawberries and cream
5. *The Hatchet*
6. *Lusitania*
7. words that suggest by their sound the idea presented
8. ampersand
9. victory that's as disastrous as a defeat
10. Park Lane and Mayfair

Test 100:

The B.A. Level

1-h	6-i
2-e	7-d
3-j	8-f
4-a	9-c
5-b	10-g

The M.S. Level

1-e	6-c
2-i	7-d
3-j	8-b
4-a	9-h
5-g	10-f

The Ph.D. Level

1-f	6-b
2-g	7-e
3-a	8-j
4-i	9-h
5-d	10-c